THE
HOLY SPIRIT

A BIBLE STUDY GUIDE FOR CATHOLICS

THE HOLY SPIRIT

A BIBLE STUDY GUIDE FOR CATHOLICS

FR. MITCH PACWA, S.J.

Our Sunday Visitor
Huntington, Indiana

Nihil Obstat
Msgr. Michael Heintz, Ph.D.
Censor Librorum

Imprimatur
✠ Kevin C. Rhoades
Bishop of Fort Wayne-South Bend
December 19, 2015

The *Nihil Obstat* and *Imprimatur* are official declarations that a book is free from doctrinal or moral error. It is not implied that those who have granted the *Nihil Obstat* and *Imprimatur* agree with the contents, opinions, or statements expressed.

ISBN: 978-1-61278-959-0 (T1726)
RELIGION/Biblical Studies/Bible Study Guides
RELIGION/Christianity/Catholic
RELIGION/Inspirational

eISBN: 978-1-61278-961-3
LCCN: 2016944025

Cover design: Chelsea Alt
Cover art: Shutterstock
Interior design: Sherri L. Hoffman
Interior art: iStockPhoto.com

PRINTED IN THE UNITED STATES OF AMERICA

CONTENTS

CONTENTS

HOW TO USE THIS STUDY GUIDE IN A GROUP

This is an interactive study guide. It can be read with profit either alone or as part of a group Bible study. Below are suggestions for the use of this book in a group.

WHAT YOU WILL NEED FOR EVERY SESSION

- This study guide
- A Bible
- A notebook

- **Before Session 1, members of the group are encouraged to read the Introduction and Session 1 and to complete all the exercises in both.** They should bring this study guide with them to the group session.
- **Begin the session with prayer** (for example, see the *Veni, Creator Spiritus* prayer on page 167.)
- **Invite one person in the group to read one of the Scripture passages included in this session's material.**
- **Allow five minutes of silent reflection on the passage.** This allows the group's members to quiet their inner thoughts and to center themselves on the lesson to be discussed.
- **Catechesis:** Give all members a chance to share some point that they have learned about the Holy Spirit. Was this something new or a new insight into something? Was there anything that raised a question? (Allow fifteen to twenty minutes for this.)
- **Discussion:** Use the discussion questions at the end of the session chapter to begin a deeper grasp of the material covered in the session. (Allow fifteen to twenty minutes for this.)

- **Conclusion:** Have all members of the group summarize the key concepts they learned about the Holy Spirit in the session. Assign the next session as homework, to be completed before the next group session.

SYMBOLS USED IN THIS STUDY GUIDE

(i) = Information

(✋) = Stop and Read

(🔍) = Investigate

(💬) = Quotation

ACKNOWLEDGMENTS

Unless otherwise noted, the Scripture citations used in this work are taken from the *Catholic Edition of* the *Revised Standard Version of the Bible* (RSV), copyright © 1965, 1966 by the Division of Christian Education of the National Council of the Churches of Christ in the United States of America. Used by permission. All rights reserved.

Where noted, other Scripture citations are from the *Revised Standard Version of the Bible — Second Catholic Edition* (Ignatius Edition), designated as RSV-SCE. Copyright © 1965, 1966, 2006 by the National Council of the Churches of Christ in the United States of America. Used by permission. All rights reserved.

Quotations from papal and other Vatican-generated documents available on vatican.va are copyright © Libreria Editrice Vaticana.

English translation of the *Catechism of the Catholic Church* for use in the United States of America copyright © 1994, United States Catholic Conference, Inc. — Libreria Editrice Vaticana. English translation of the *Catechism of the Catholic Church: Modifications from the Editio Typica* copyright © 1997, United States Catholic Conference, Inc. — Libreria Editrice Vaticana.

English translation of the Nicene Creed by the English Language Liturgical Consultation (ELLC).

Excerpts from the English translation of *The Liturgy of the Hours*, © 1973, 1974, 1975, International Commission on English in the Liturgy Corporation (ICEL). All rights reserved.

INTRODUCTION

 "O Holy Spirit, descend plentifully into my heart. Enlighten the dark corners of this neglected dwelling, and scatter there Thy cheerful beams."

— St. Augustine

The *Catechism of the Catholic Church* says that

> "Holy Spirit" is the proper name of the one whom we adore and glorify with the Father and the Son. The Church has received this name from the Lord and professes it in the Baptism of her new children. (CCC 691)

This Bible study looks at the Holy Spirit in Scripture, beginning with the Old Testament and moving through the New Testament. In seven sessions, we examine: the role of the Holy Spirit in creation; how authority and power come from the Spirit; how the Spirit worked in the lives of the prophets; the Spirit as the giver of wisdom, guidance, and truth; the Spirit as part of the Trinity; empowerment and the Spirit; and finally, the Spirit in lives of Christian believers.

It is our hope that this Bible study will encourage all of us — in the words of the *Veni, Creator Spiritus*, which dates back to the ninth century — to ask the Holy Spirit, "In our hearts take up Thy rest."

Session 1

THE HOLY SPIRIT IN CREATION

> "The Holy Spirit, then, as Jesus promises, guides us 'into all truth' (Jn 16:13). He leads us not only to an encounter with Jesus, the fullness of Truth, but guides us 'into' the Truth, that is, he helps us enter into a deeper communion with Jesus himself, gifting us knowledge of the things of God."
>
> — POPE FRANCIS, General Audience (May 15, 2013)

Just as the whole of the Bible opens with creation and its first mention of the Spirit of God, so will this study begin with examining passages in five books of the Old Testament that present the role of the Holy Spirit in creation. The importance of this doctrine is shown in that it appears in narrative books (Genesis and Judith), a prophetic book (Ezekiel), a psalm, and a wisdom book (Wisdom of Solomon). The diversity of literature indicates that the link between God's Spirit and creation took deep roots in all sectors of Israelite thinking, especially after the exile.

STUDY

Genesis

The Old Testament does not use the phrase "Holy Spirit" very often, but it does speak frequently of the "Spirit of God" or "Spirit of the Lord." In fact, the account of the creation of the universe contains the first reference to the "Spirit of God."

15

> Stop here and read **Genesis 1:1-3** in your own Bible.

Genesis opens with the claim that God "created" the heavens and the earth. The word meaning "create" occurs about a hundred times in the Old Testament. However, only God is the "creator," and never is this action shared by anyone else.

Using some terminology from Babylonian myths, the earth is described as a primeval chaos, translated here as "without form and void" (Gen 1:2) and absolutely dark over a vast abyss. The Babylonian myth portrays "formless" and "void" as the parent gods of everything, but Scripture demythologizes them into mere natural forces. While

BABYLONIAN CREATION MYTH

The Babylonian creation myth, *Enuma Elish*, begins with the Father god Apsu, who was fresh water, and the Mother goddess Tiamat, who was salt water. They procreate children gods, each of whom is a force of nature. Apsu hates their noisiness and decides to kill them, so Tiamat incites the wind god to kill Apsu by freezing him — thereby explaining the Ice Age and polar cap. Then Tiamat fears that her children will kill *her*, and so she creates a monster, Kingu, to kill them. The children ask the storm god, Marduk, to be their king, and he leads them in battle, killing both Tiamat and Kingu.

Marduk cuts Tiamat's corpse in two, the long way, making the earth from her bottom half and the sky from the top. The Tigris and Euphrates rivers flow from her eyes, while the sun, moon, and stars hang on her rib cage like a track lighting system, controlling the "destinies of gods and men" (this is the origin of astrology). Marduk cuts off Kingu's head, mixes his blood with the earth, and makes human beings into the slaves of the gods, forcing them to feed the gods by offering sacrifices to keep them nourished. In that light, read all of Genesis 1 and contrast the two versions of creation, especially the role of the sun, moon, and stars, the sea monsters, and the purpose of human beings.

the Babylonian myth tells of the wind god killing his grandfather Apsu — the Abyss of fresh water — by freezing him, Scripture (in Hebrew) describes how the "Spirit of God hovers" over this chaos. Just as the eagle "flutters" or "hovers" (same Hebrew word) to draw eaglets out of the nest to try to fly, so does the Spirit of God "move above" or "hover" over the chaos in order to prepare it for God's next step of speaking everything into existence: "God said, 'Let there be ...' "

In the Gospel of John, the prologue starts like Genesis 1:1, in order to draw attention to Christ's divinity: "In the beginning was the Word, and the Word was with God, and the Word was God. He was in the beginning with God; all things were made through him, and without him was not anything made that was made" (Jn 1:1-3).

Not only does the text explicitly say "the Word was God" but also that he has his role in the creation of the universe: "All things were made through him, and without him was not anything made that was made." John is hereby saying that when God "said" in order to create, his word was the second Person of the Holy Trinity.

When Christians read Genesis 1:1-3 and John 1:1-3, they then recognize that all three Persons were intimately involved in the creation of the world: God the Father speaks creation into being; the Son is the Word through whom all things come to be; and the Holy Spirit hovers over chaos in order to draw forth from it the potential by which the Word gives it form, shape, principles of motion, and any other elements of being a creature. With such reflection in mind, it is no surprise that some of the Fathers of the Church saw the Blessed Trinity being prefigured in Genesis 1:26: "God said, 'Let us make man in our image, after our likeness.' " The first-person plural "us" and "our" hinted at the three divine Persons, but only the revelation made by Jesus Christ could clarify its meaning.

CONSIDER

Psalm 104

Ancient Israel had a very positive attitude toward creation — God created it himself, and he declared all of his creatures to be good. Psalm 104 praises God for his creation and its orderly structure, encouraging amazement at creation's wonder so as to learn to live wisely in accord with its good order. The role of God's Spirit enters when the psalm describes God's determination of death and life.

 Stop here and read **Psalm 104** (especially verses 29 and 30) in your own Bible.

Here we see the role of the Spirit in the life and death of every living thing. When the Lord sends his Spirit, life comes and living beings are created. As in Genesis, the coming of the Spirit precedes the acts of creation, but appears as a necessary, preparatory step. The only difference here is that the Spirit is engaged in the ongoing work of creation, even at very small, individual levels, making possible the ongoing renewal of the face of the earth.

Ezekiel

Ezekiel and thousands of others had been taken prisoner to Babylon in 598 B.C., the first time King Nebuchadnezzar subdued the Kingdom of Judah. Throughout his exile, Ezekiel kept warning Judah to repent or be destroyed. Just as they had failed to listen to Jeremiah, they refused his warnings. Nonetheless, like Jeremiah, when Ezekiel learned that Jerusalem had been completely destroyed in 587 B.C., he never gloated. Rather, the Lord sent him a series of prophecies and visions of a new future. One of the best known is his vision of the valley of dry bones, over which he prophesies. The bones are rejoined, sinews and flesh come upon them, and then he prophesies to the breath to return to these dead people and bring them to life.

 Stop here and read **Ezekiel 37:1-14** in your own Bible.

Though the exiles felt as good as dead because they were without any hope, the Lord gave them a vision of hope through Ezekiel: the

Spirit of the Lord can bring forth life even out of a vast valley filled with death. In 37:14, the Lord explains, "I will put my Spirit within you, and you shall live." The Spirit of the Lord makes it possible even for dried-up and scattered bones to live, demonstrating the role of the Spirit in creation and re-creation. The life-giving role of the Lord's Spirit occurs when the prophet speaks and makes possible the action of the Spirit, showing that the creative and prophetic roles belong together.

Judith

Judith 16:1-17 is a hymn of thanksgiving for the way the Lord delivered Israel from the invading army of Holofernes. As in Psalm 104:30, the Lord's Spirit is sent out by him to form creatures.

 Stop here and read **Judith 16:1-17** in your own Bible.

The purpose of this hymn is to praise God for his salvation of Israel during the crisis of the invasion of the land by Holofernes. As part of that "new song" (Jud 16:13), all creatures are summoned to serve the Lord, their creator. As in Genesis, God speaks all the creatures into being, but God also sends his Spirit, who formed the creatures. At the same time, the Spirit of God helps the creatures hear God's voice, and the formation of creatures by the Spirit makes it hard for them to resist the call of God's voice. This passage links the Spirit's role in forming creatures with the power of God's word to create them and the power of his word to summon them to perform his will. This latter function is a connection between the Spirit's creative role and his role with the prophets.

STUDY

Book of Wisdom

One last book treats of the role of the Lord's Spirit in creation: the Book of Wisdom. This was written in Greek, probably in Alexandria,

Egypt, in the first century B.C. Wisdom identifies the Spirit of the Lord as the one who fills the whole world and sustains all things in existence.

INVESTIGATE

Look up the following passages and make notes on the role of the Lord's Spirit.

PASSAGE	NOTES
Wisdom 1:7-8	
Wisdom 12:1-2	

The first reading takes the creative power of the Spirit of the Lord to two other levels. The first level claims that the Spirit of the Lord continuously and in an ongoing way sustains all that has already been created. He did not simply give it an original start but is constantly bestowing new life. The second level claims that the Spirit of the Lord is also able to know everything that people say and speak. He notices all unrighteousness, judges it, and punishes it.

Two more passages in Wisdom express the ongoing presence of the Lord's Spirit in all of creation and the effects of the Spirit to maintain all of reality. Wisdom 12:1-2 simply offers an acknowledgment to God that his Spirit is a moral presence throughout all of creation. Being everywhere and within all things indicates the divine quality of the Lord's Spirit. God's infinite nature is omnipresent and is within everything that exists. This teaching is not the same as pantheism, which claims that everything *is* God. God is the creator of everything, and even his action of creating is one that only God does; everything else is a creature that is limited in space and time, and an infinite gap exists between the creatures and the infinite, uncreated, and eternal God. At the same time, all of creation and everything within creation is sustained in existence by the infinite presence of God. He is within everything, and yet without being merely one thing among the rest of creatures. He sustains all creatures, but they do not sustain him in the least.

The passage further reveals that the omnipresence of the Spirit of the Lord goes beyond simply sustaining all creation. The Spirit also corrects human beings when they sin against God. The goal of his moral correction is that "they may be freed from wickedness and put their trust in you, O Lord" (Wis 12:2, RSV-SCE). Jesus will teach that the Holy Spirit of truth will have the same role of correcting people about "sin and righteousness and judgment" (Jn 16:8; also see Jn 16:9-11). In this way, Wisdom indicates that moral virtue and faith are linked to each other, and that both are connected to the action of the Spirit of the Lord acting within creation. People cannot claim to have faith and yet ignore their need for moral improvement. Such is God's way of leading and guiding people ever closer to himself.

CONSIDER

Wisdom 7:21-30 is a statement that flows from the secrets learned from wisdom about a Spirit that permeates wisdom itself, all other spirits (including the human spirits), and everything else that exists.

The first important point is to accept that the Spirit is capable of penetrating wisdom itself. In saying this, the Book of Wisdom is recognizing that the Spirit is superior to wisdom. Also, the Spirit is able to penetrate all "intelligent and pure and most subtle" spirits (Wis 7:23). This indicates that he is superior to the angels, who are super-intelligent, pure spirits. He is superior to human spirits, who are intelligent, though less intelligent and less pure than the angels. The obvious conclusion one should draw from this teaching is that human spirits should have at least as much respect for God's Spirit as do the angels, especially since human intelligence and goodness is so inferior to the angels, yet alone God's Spirit. Having asserted that the Spirit is superior to wisdom, and to angelic and human spirits, the sage then lists some of the qualities of this Spirit.

INVESTIGATE

QUALITIES OF THE SPIRIT

Read **Wisdom 7:22-30** and list the qualities of the Spirit.

_____

_____

_____

_____

_____

_____

_____

_____

_____

_____

   Each quality bears reflection to help us deepen our understanding of the Spirit of the Lord. Some of the characteristics are intellectual — as when the Spirit is described as *intelligent, manifold,* and *keen.* Some characteristics are moral qualities — *holy, unpolluted, loving the good.* Some characteristics belong more to the divine nature — *invulnerable, irresistible, all-powerful.* Human beings cannot fully understand these characteristics, but they can consider them prayerfully and meditatively so as to grow in wonder and awe at the greatness of God's Holy Spirit. This is a way to avoid taking him for granted or thinking we are more intelligent than he.

DISCUSS
   1. What was, and still is, the role of the Spirit in creation?
   2. Which of the Old Testament passages you've read this week gave you new insights into the Holy Spirit?
   3. What quality of the Holy Spirit do you wish to incorporate into your daily life?

PRACTICE
This week, think about how the Holy Spirit is active in the creation of your life. What areas of your being need the enlightenment and work of the Spirit to activate them? How can you live a richer and fuller life with the assistance of the Spirit? Choose one of the qualities of the Spirit and look for ways to bring it to life in your own life over the next few days.

Session 2

AUTHORITY AND POWER COME BY THE HOLY SPIRIT

> "The Church, therefore, instructed by the words of Christ, and drawing on the experience of Pentecost and her own apostolic history, has proclaimed since the earliest centuries her faith in the Holy Spirit, as the giver of life, the one in whom the inscrutable Triune God communicates himself to human beings, constituting in them the source of eternal life."
>
> — POPE ST. JOHN PAUL II, *Dominum et Vivificantem* (n. 1)

Another very distinct theme in the Old Testament is that the Spirit of God grants authority to various human beings, either to hold particular offices or to have particular powers. This will be a very important background and prefiguring for the New Testament teaching on the Holy Spirit as the source of gifts, or charisms, in the Church. In this session, we will be looking at how the Holy Spirit dealt with Joshua, Moses' successor; the judges, the rulers of Israel; and the kings of Israel.

Joshua

The Lord God had famously called Moses from the burning bush to lead Israel to freedom from slavery in Egypt. This was a unique role and not a hereditary or elected office or institution. Still, after Moses died, someone needed to lead the people of Israel into the Promised Land. That role fell to a younger man — Joshua, son of

Nun — who had been at his side in various roles from the time right after the people's escape from Egypt.

INVESTIGATE

JOSHUA AND THE WILDERNESS

Look up the following passages and note Joshua's actions.

PASSAGE	NOTES
Exodus 17:1-14	
Exodus 24:13-14	
Exodus 32:17-18	
Exodus 33:11	

Numbers 11:27-29	
Numbers 13:1-16	
Numbers 14:1-38	

STUDY

Throughout the wandering in the wilderness, Joshua showed himself to be courageous in battle, loyal to Moses, and faithful to and trusting in the Lord. The Lord's choice of Joshua to lead Israel was not a reward but the result of Joshua having proven himself capable of the role through his previous actions, virtues, and faith.

Two passages depict the choice of Joshua as Moses' successor in leading Israel: one before Moses died and one after. At both stages, the role of the Spirit of God is key.

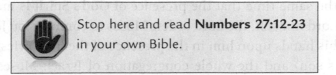

Stop here and read **Numbers 27:12-23** in your own Bible.

The passage opens with the Lord's command that Moses go up another mountain, this time to see the Promised Land before he dies. Moses had failed to obey the Lord's command to speak to the rock in order to make water flow out for the people (see Num 20:8-13). The nature of this sin derived from the Lord's intention to bring water out by his word rather than by Moses' act of striking the rock; the people might think Moses' action brought out the water, when it was the power of the Lord's word. Moses failed to obey God and thus failed to give the people an important teaching moment about the authority of God's word. Therefore, he will be permitted to see the Promised Land but not to enter it. At this point, Moses petitions the Lord to appoint another man to lead the people of Israel after him:

> Moses said to the LORD, "Let the LORD, the God of the spirits of all flesh, appoint a man over the congregation, who shall go out before them and come in before them, who shall lead them out and bring them in; that the congregation of the LORD may not be as sheep which have no shepherd." (Num 27:15-17).

The Lord is identified as the "God of the spirits of all flesh," echoing a similar expression in Job 12:10: "In his hand is the soul of every living thing and the spirit of all mankind" (author's translation). The reason for Moses to include this description here is that he wants the Lord to appoint a well-qualified leader. This will not be defined merely by external accomplishments but by the inner spirit of a man, which only the Lord can know. The Lord responds positively to Moses' request by naming Joshua the son of Nun.

Not only does the Lord know Joshua's spirit, as he knows the spirits of all people, but he also knows that "the Spirit" — that is, the Spirit of God — is upon him. The presence of God's Spirit will be a key qualification for Joshua to lead the people morally as well as militarily and organizationally.

At the same time that the presence of God's Spirit is made clear by the Lord himself, the Lord orders Moses to commission Joshua by laying his hands upon him in the presence of the high priest Eleazar (Aaron's son) and the whole congregation of Israel. Moses confers some of his authority upon Joshua by the laying on of hands, but the high priest and the people are present to signal their approval of Joshua and therefore their willingness to follow and obey him. In this scene, we see that the special gift of the Spirit is bestowed, along with the ceremonial and liturgical actions of approval. Even though the Lord bestows the Spirit, as only the Lord can, the liturgical celebration of this office is very important to the life of the nation.

Stop here and read **Deuteronomy 34:7-12** in your own Bible.

This text begins at the death of Moses at 120 years of age and the thirty-day period of grieving for him. At the end of this period, Joshua takes up the leadership role he was chosen to have about five weeks earlier. Briefly, the text notes that Joshua takes up the reins and the people obey him, as the Lord commanded Moses. Yet note that Joshua is also described as having God's Spirit, who is characterized by wisdom. The ways Joshua lives under the influence of the Spirit of wisdom will be demonstrated throughout the Book of Joshua. It is worth noting the epilogue to this notification about Joshua's leadership:

> And there has not arisen a prophet since in Israel like Moses, whom the LORD knew face to face, none like him for all the signs and the wonders which the LORD sent him to do in the land of Egypt, to Pharaoh and to all his servants and to all his land, and for all the mighty power and all the great and terrible deeds which Moses wrought in the sight of all Israel. (Deut 34:10-12).

As filled with the Spirit of wisdom that Joshua might be, he still does not equal Moses for two key reasons: Moses knew the Lord "face to face," thereby making him the greatest of all prophets; and no one did miracles as Moses did, with mighty power and great wonder. Christians might consider this from the perspective that Jesus (in Hebrew Jehoshua or Jeshua, a form of Joshua) will exceed Moses both in his knowledge of God (from all eternity as God's only begotten Son) as well as the many miracles he performed, most especially his resurrection from the dead — Moses still remains dead. An interesting comparison indeed.

Judges

Modern readers understand the term "judge" primarily through the lens of the law court and the respect due to those addressed as "Your Honor" because they adjudicate cases. However, the Hebrew term *shafat* and its Ugaritic equivalent *th-ph-t* include the sense of ruling people as well as adjudicating cases in court. The Book of Judges relates the stories of such leaders in Israel, roughly from 1200 B.C. to 1050 B.C., a period of political insecurity throughout the Middle East that affected the tribes of Israel as they settled into the land of Canaan, the land promised to their ancestors Abraham, Isaac, and Jacob.

THE WORLD OF THE JUDGES

Egypt had reached the pinnacle of its power under Rameses II, considered by a majority of scholars as the pharaoh of the Exodus period. After many wars in Canaan and elsewhere, Rameses died in 1212 B.C., after a sixty-seven-year reign, and was succeeded by a son, Merneptah, who mentioned defeating Israel in a battle in 1207 B.C. His first successors were not strong until Rameses III, who defeated a Philistine invasion of Egypt and forced them to settle in Canaan as agents of the Egyptian Empire in 1178 B.C. These iron-smelting tribes from the Mediterranean islands caused Israel much trouble during the period of the Judges and the time of King David. Other tribes were very active, particularly the Moabites and Edomites, who were Bedouin tribes settling in the territory of modern Jordan, east of Israel. They fought the Egyptians and Israelites alike in an attempt to gain control over the land of Canaan. Such is the background of the chaotic world of the judges.

In addition to the political turmoil caused by the increasing weakness of Egypt, the Hittite Empire, and the Assyrian Empire, the Israelites brought chaos upon themselves by worshiping the pagan deities Baal and Anath, despite the first commandment to have "no other gods before me" (Ex 20:3). Israel's spiritual weakness typically led to attacks and invasions by the Philistines, Moabites, Edomites, and others, which the Israelites understood as the Lord's punishment for their sins. At those points, they cried out for help, and the Lord sent them judges.

The chronology of the judges adds up to 400 years, which is longer than most scholars would grant to the period of the judges. The best explanation is that the judges ruled in different tribes of Israel, as the text says. It is fairly likely that they overlapped one another in time, though in different parts of the country, making possible the occurrence of their deeds and rule within the 150 years or so between Joshua and King Saul.

INVESTIGATE

THE SPIRIT OF THE LORD

 Look up the following passages and make notes on who is involved and how the Spirit of the Lord came upon them before reading the explanations below.

PASSAGE	NOTES
Judges 3:8-10	
Judges 6:33-35	
Judges 11:29-40	

STUDY

Othniel

The Israelites worshiped Baal and the female Asheroth deities of Canaan, so the Lord allowed them to be invaded by Cushan-rishathaim from Aram of the two rivers — that is, northern Mesopotamia. Othniel was from Judah, and therefore far to the south of Aram (modern-day Syria). When Israel repented of worshiping Canaanite gods, the Lord raised up Othniel by pouring his Spirit upon him. The Spirit made Othniel into a military leader able to defeat Cushan-rishathaim and deliver Israel. After that, Israel was at peace for forty years until Othniel died.

Gideon

Again Israel sinned, so the Lord allowed the Midianites — a Bedouin tribe that had conquered the area of modern Jordan south of Amman, along the east side of the Dead Sea — to attack. Before the Israelites met the Midianites in battle, the Spirit of the Lord "clothed" (literal translation of the Hebrew) Gideon, strengthening him to sound a trumpet call to all the tribes to help attack the Midianites and Amalekites.

This empowerment stands in stark contrast to Gideon's self-description at his call by an angel, "Pray, Lord, how can I deliver Israel? Behold, my clan is the weakest in Manasseh, and I am the least in my family" (Judg 6:15). Manasseh was the youngest tribe, Gideon's Abiezrite clan was the least clan in Manasseh, and he was the least member of his clan. This means that Gideon was at the very bottom of the Israelite totem pole, the man with the least status in the whole nation. Yet the Lord's Spirit was powerful enough to transform even Gideon into a warrior capable of driving out the oppressive raiders.

Jephthah

Like Gideon, Jephthah was extremely low in the social order of Israel. His father was called Gilead, the name of the Jordanian plateau north of Amman, and his mother was an unnamed prostitute. His father's legitimate sons drove him away from the family to the arid region northeast of Gilead, where he gathered a group of fellow outsiders and bandits. However, the Ammonites attacked the Israelite tribes living east of the Jordan River. At that point, the Israelites living on the Gilead plateau begged Jephthah to lead them, to which, after some negotiations, he agreed. Next, he tried negotiation with the Ammonites, but these negotiations failed, so war became inevitable.

Before Jephthah began his march to battle, the "Spirit of the LORD" came upon him (Judg 11:29), enabling him to lead the eastern Israelite tribes to victory. However, he did not receive the gift of wisdom, since he made an open-ended vow to sacrifice the first one who came out to meet him — probably assuming it would be one of the domestic animals. Tragically, his only daughter came out first, so he sacrificed her, much to his and her lament (Judg 11:32-40).

Samson

Samson is regarded as the last of the major judges.

INVESTIGATE

THE STORY OF SAMSON

 Look up the following passages and make notes about Samson before reading the explanation below.

PASSAGE	NOTES
Judges 13:24-25	
Judges 14:5-6, 18-20	

Judges 15:14-15	
Judges 16	

A childless woman of the tribe of Dan was approached by an angel of the Lord with a promise that she would bear a son who would save the southern tribes from the Philistines. The angel confirmed this message to her doubting husband, Manoah. At this point, the Danites still lived in the south, near Judah and Simeon, but closer to the Philistines living on the southern coastal plane in five cities along the Mediterranean Sea. The Philistines had brought iron smelting to the region and maintained a monopoly on iron in a region where people knew how to smelt copper and tin, which were used to make the alloy called bronze. Iron was stronger than bronze, giving the Philistines a technological advantage over Israel.

Though Dan was a small tribe that would eventually be forced to move to the far north of the country due to their military weakness in the face of the Philistine threat, the Spirit of the Lord would come upon one warrior and use him to punish the Philistines. As with Jephthah, the Spirit of the Lord gave young Samson great strength to fight the Philistines on his own, but he was not very wise in his general conduct.

Samson desired to marry a Philistine woman, despite his parents' objections to marrying a non-Israelite. On the way to the marriage, at Timnah, the Spirit of the Lord came so mightily upon him that he was able to tear apart a lion. From seeing the carcass of that lion filled with bees and honey, he composed a riddle for the guests at his wedding. They cheated in solving the riddle, leading him to kill thirty Philistine men in their city of Ashkelon so that he could pay those who solved the riddle. However, he lost his wife to his best man because of killing the thirty Philistines. Samson was physically strengthened by the Lord's Spirit, but not made wise.

Samson's next adventure started with a failed attempt to reconcile with his estranged wife. In revenge for not getting his wife back, he set the tails of 300 foxes on fire and let the crazed animals run through the Philistine fields and crops. The Philistines retaliated against Judah with war, so the Judahites convinced Samson to be bound and handed over to the Philistines at the town of Lehi. At that point, the Spirit of the Lord came upon him so powerfully that he snapped the ropes holding him, grabbed the jawbone of a dead ass, and killed the Philistine soldiers with it.

Samson never became very wise. His final adventures began with a fatal attraction to a prostitute in Gaza named Delilah. Though her first two attempts to trick him to reveal the secret of his strength failed, her third succeeded. The Philistines overpowered him, blinded him, and made him a slave. In one final, fatal retaliation, the blind Samson knocked down the main supporting pillars of the Philistine temple, killing many of them and himself in the process. Clearly he was strong but never wise.

CONSIDER

The Kings and the Spirit of the Lord

In the time of the judges, the Spirit of the Lord strengthened each of them to save Israel from one of the many enemies in the area, in response to the people's repentance for sin and the Lord's decision to show them mercy. However, most of the judges were local, capable of leading one or a few tribes but not all of Israel. Further, they were able to muster local militias but not any standing armies ready to defend the nation from attackers. Nor did they establish a dynasty or some other institution of ongoing leadership.

In the middle of the eleventh century B.C., Samuel was a combination prophet and judge, but his sons were too corrupt to continue his service to the nation. The people clamored for a king in 1 Samuel 8, and the Lord permitted it, guiding Samuel to choose and anoint Saul as the first king and then get popular support for his leadership (1 Sam 9-10). The first crisis arose when the Ammonites besieged the town of Jabesh-gilead, a town somewhere along modern Wadi el-Jabis, which flows from the Gilead plateau in Jordan down to the Jordan River.

 Stop here and read **1 Samuel 11:1-7** in your own Bible.

When the Spirit of God "rushed" ("came mightily" is a bit interpretive) upon Saul at hearing the plea of the threatened people of Jabesh-gilead, his anger was "kindled," or became hot (1 Sam 11:6). His action of cutting two oxen into pieces to be sent throughout the land of Israel as a threat to those who refuse to help save Jabesh-gilead was a symbol for those who belonged to the national covenant. People who broke covenants were threatened with being cut to pieces, and that was the nature of Saul's threat. Of course, the people responded and saved Jabesh-gilead. Years later, when the Philistines hanged Saul's decapitated body on the walls of Beth-shan, the men of Jabesh-gilead took it down at night and buried it honorably in repayment.

STUDY

King Saul did not always obey the word of the Lord, and the prophet Samuel informed him that his kingdom was to be removed from him and his family (1 Sam 15). Therefore, the Lord sent Samuel to anoint a new king in Bethlehem. He examined the sons of Jesse, until the Lord chose the youngest son, David, but not on the basis of his strength, height, or good looks — characteristics that had impressed the historian in regard to Saul, as well as Samuel and the people, and had impressed Samuel about David's older brothers. Rather, the Lord looked on the heart and designated David, who also happened to be handsome and ruddy in appearance:

Then Samuel took the horn of oil, and anointed him in the midst of his brothers; and the Spirit of the LORD came mightily upon David from that day forward. And Samuel rose up, and went to Ramah. Now the Spirit of the LORD departed from Saul, and an evil spirit from the LORD tormented him. (1 Sam 16:13-14)

Somewhat parallel to the laying of hands on Joshua in the religious assembly, the Spirit of the Lord "rushed upon" David as Samuel anointed him "in the midst of his brothers" during a peace-offering sacrifice. Though the Spirit rushed upon David, no specific attitude or action is described in connection with this gift of the Spirit; his effects will have to be seen as David's life and reign unfold over the coming years. The text also says that the Spirit of the Lord "departed" from Saul, upon whom the Lord's Spirit had rushed at the beginning of his reign. Saul is not left in a neutral spiritual state, but an evil spirit has taken the place of the Lord's Spirit. Like nature, the supernatural does not like a vacuum. The effects of Saul's evil spirit will be manifest as he tries to kill David, and even his own son.

Even though the Lord did not want the people to have a king with a standing army, military draft, and large government bureaucracy, he nonetheless sent his own Spirit to empower the first two kings to be able to do their missions of leading Israel. Yet the presence of the Spirit of the Lord depended on the fidelity of the king to doing the Lord's will and avoiding sin. The active role of the Spirit depends on fidelity to God's moral law, as Saul learns to his chagrin.

CONSIDER

 Stop here and read **1 Chronicles 12:16-18** in your own Bible.

The Chronicles retell much of the history of the kings of Israel and Judah, often using the material in the Books of Samuel and Kings, but also drawing on other traditions and records. One interesting notice about the role of the Spirit occurs after Saul had died in battle with the Philistines and after all the tribes assembled at the city of Hebron (meaning "Confederacy" in Hebrew) to anoint David king, not only of Judah but of all twelve tribes. Various warriors assembled to pledge loyalty to David from each of the tribes, including Benjamin, which was the tribe of King Saul. They required special attention because of their natural inclination to remain loyal to Saul, their now dead tribesman and former enemy of David. David meets them with a special offer, that if they have come in friendship, his "heart will be knit" (1 Chron 12:17) to them.

Amasai, the chief of thirty elite Benjaminite warriors, is "clothed" with the Spirit and makes his pledge of loyalty and peace to David and his assistants. This clothing with the Spirit of God makes it possible for these warriors to overcome the natural loyalties of tribe and kinship with Saul so that they can join the new king, David, who had also been endowed with the same Spirit of the Lord at his secret anointing by Samuel.

STUDY

The political leadership within Israel is understood to be instituted and guided by the Lord's Spirit from the time of Joshua through the time of the first kings, Saul and David. Because of their sins, their successors are not portrayed as being so filled with the Spirit. In fact, their sins are included in Israel's royal histories with an honesty rarely seen among their neighboring kingdoms. This history points out that the institution of leadership might be begun with the Spirit, but the sins of the people can make them incapable of sensitivity to his divine influence. Even when someone like Saul has the Spirit rush upon him, he can lose the presence of the Lord's Spirit because of his disobedience to God's commands. Human inconstancy is a serious issue in their life of the Spirit, such that sin might block his actions and cut off the life of the Spirit.

Recall the Book of Wisdom on the Lord's Spirit and judgment of people:

For your immortal spirit is in all things.
Therefore you correct little by little those who trespass,
and remind and warn them of the things wherein they sin,
that they may be freed from wickedness and put their trust in
   you, O Lord. (Wis 12:1-2)

The Spirit of the Lord works to correct the people of Israel for their national sins, especially of idolatry, and the sins of the kings, especially disobedience. It is not farfetched to think that Wisdom 12:1-2 may be a reflection how individuals and institutions who were inspired by the Spirit of the Lord can go wrong due to human sin, and the same Spirit will bring the correction. Every human, especially those who claim to have Spirit-inspired authority, must stay extra alert to their responsibilities lest their trust in the Lord sour into self-confidence that precedes their downfall, as with Saul and others.

DISCUSS

1. What differences do you see between the action of the Lord's Spirit in the Old Testament and the Holy Spirit in the New Testament?
2. How can someone have the Lord's Spirit for power but not wisdom (see Samson)?
3. What is the relationship between the Spirit and human sin?

PRACTICE

This week, think about how the Holy Spirit acted in the lives of Old Testament figures. What aspects of the Holy Spirit that were shown in the Old Testament can you see in your life or the lives of believers around you? How can you more fully develop the wisdom and power offered by the Spirit in your life? Consider if it is possible that some sin might be blocking the power of the Spirit to work through you.

Session 3

PROPHETS AND THE SPIRIT OF GOD

> "Breathe in me, O Holy Spirit, that my thoughts may all be holy. Act in me, O Holy Spirit, that my work, too, may be holy. Draw my heart, O Holy Spirit, that I love but what is holy. Strengthen me, O Holy Spirit, to defend all that is holy. Guard me, then, O Holy Spirit, that I always may be holy. Amen."
>
> — St. Augustine

A rather odd beginning to the study of the role of the Spirit of God among the prophets is Balaam the son of Beor, the first prophet mentioned in the Bible to have "the Spirit of God [come] upon him" (Num 24:2). What makes this so odd is that Balaam lived "at Pethor, which is near the River, in the land of Amaw" (Num 22:5), which was ancient Pitru on the Euphrates River, twelve miles south of Carchemish, a city in the pagan region of Mesopotamia. In other words, Balaam was a pagan prophet who had been summoned by Balak, king of Moab, to curse Israel (Num 22:2-7).

At first, God forbids Balaam to go, but then, after King Balak sends a second delegation of even more important nobles to plead with him, God does permit it, on the condition that Balaam speak only what God gives him to say. On the way south to Moab, Balaam's ass sees an angel blocking the road and stops his progress three times until Balaam can also see the angel. The angel repeats that Balaam can only speak what God tells him to say, and Balaam makes that point with Balak before offering sacrifices prior to speaking his words.

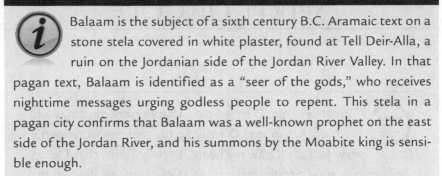

"A SEER OF THE GODS"

Balaam is the subject of a sixth century B.C. Aramaic text on a stone stela covered in white plaster, found at Tell Deir-Alla, a ruin on the Jordanian side of the Jordan River Valley. In that pagan text, Balaam is identified as a "seer of the gods," who receives nighttime messages urging godless people to repent. This stela in a pagan city confirms that Balaam was a well-known prophet on the east side of the Jordan River, and his summons by the Moabite king is sensible enough.

Balaam speaks four different oracles, just as "the LORD put a word" in his mouth (Num 23:5). Each oracle is a blessing on Israel, rather than the curse sought by King Balak, prompting Balak's growing anger and fear.

Stop here and read **Numbers 23:27-30, 24:1-4, 10-14,** and **25:5-9, 15-18** in your own Bible.

The Spirit of God then comes upon Balaam, and he takes "up his discourse" (Num 23:7). This description of Balaam receiving his fourth and final oracle begins with Balaam telling King Balak to prepare seven altars and sacrifices — a rejection of the typical pagan prophet looking for omens, such as patterns in the flight of birds or the position of the fat attached to the livers of the sacrificed animals, which was very popular in Mesopotamia and elsewhere. Instead, Balaam looks toward Israel's camp, and "the Spirit of God came upon him" (Num 24:2). In the first two oracles, "the LORD put a word" in his mouth; here God's Spirit comes upon him more directly. In that Spirit, Balaam "hears the words of God" and "sees the vision of the

Almighty" (Num 24:4), and he then speaks the greatest of his four oracles blessing Israel. Even when Balak's anger interrupts him, he continues on with even stronger words for Israel and against the pagan tribes of Moab, Sheth, and Seir.

Though Balaam was a pagan, he was subject to speaking the Lord's words and to the influence of God's Spirit. This will be the criterion of all true prophecies and prophets in Israel from Balaam forward.

STUDY

The Books of Samuel

The Spirit of God comes upon prophets only twice in the Books of Samuel, where the focus is much more on the role of the Spirit with the early kings Saul and David. On two occasions, the prophets do not speak oracles or give messages but act ecstatically. Both of these episodes were recorded primarily because they involved King Saul, once in a positive light and then in a negative light.

The first mention of the Spirit of the Lord is in 1 Samuel 10:5-7, immediately after Samuel the prophet anoints Saul king. Samuel gives three signs from God that Saul has been chosen as king (see 1 Sam 10:2-4 for the first two), the third of which speaks of Saul receiving the Spirit of the Lord to prophesy.

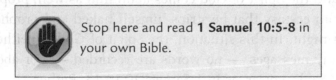

Stop here and read **1 Samuel 10:5-8** in your own Bible.

Saul is promised that the "Spirit of the LORD will come mightily upon" him, not so much to rule as to prophesy and "be turned into another man" — that is, enter an ecstatic state (1 Sam 10:6). Saul first receives the Spirit of the Lord to bestow prophetic ability on him as a sign that he is king. It is not at all directly related to his capacity to rule the people. This may be the case because the monarchy is such a new institution. Only later, in 1 Samuel 11:6, does the Spirit of the Lord come mightily upon Saul to empower him to be a king who rallies the tribes and leads them in battle to protect the town of Jabesh from Ammonite invaders coming from their main city (modern Amman — named after these Ammonites). In 1 Samuel 10:10-13, the Spirit of the Lord gives him ecstasy as a sign and nothing more lasting. Nothing is said about any words he prophesied. The only result is that the people observe it and make a proverb about their king entering the prophetic ecstasy, even though he is now accepted as their ruler.

A second similar experience occurs years later when Saul has been taken over by an evil spirit (1 Samuel 16:14) and is seeking to kill David and his men.

 Stop here and read **1 Samuel 20-24** in your own Bible.

In this case, the Spirit of God that was manifest among the prophets led by Samuel now fall upon a first and a second set of messengers who have been dispatched by Saul to capture David. The prophetic Spirit so takes control of them that they cannot fulfill their assigned task of taking David. Finally, Saul himself goes looking for David, and the Spirit of God comes upon him as well, prophesying in such an ecstasy that he strips himself naked and prophesies all day and night. In this situation, the Spirit of God is neither about giving any messages — no words are recorded — nor about augmenting Saul's power, as in 1 Samuel 10:10-13. Rather, the Spirit of God uses the ecstasy to prevent Saul from apprehending and harming David, whose gift of the Spirit is helping him lead Israel.

The Books of Kings

These books include much more material about the prophets, especially about Elijah and Elisha. The Spirit of God does not come prophetically upon the kings in these books as he did in 1 Samuel, upon Saul and David. However, on three occasions, the Spirit of God does come upon three prophets: Elijah, Elisha, and Micaiah ben Imlah (Micaiah the son of Imlah).

STUDY

Micaiah ben Imlah

The second mention of the Spirit of the Lord concerns a prophet contemporary with Elisha — Micaiah ben Imlah.

 Stop here and read **1 Kings 22:1-28** in your own Bible.

The situation is that Jehoshaphat, king of Judah, and Ahab, king of Israel, decide to fight a campaign against Syria to retake the Israelite city of Ramothgilead (now in modern Jordan). Jehoshaphat asks to consult the prophets of the Lord but is dissatisfied with their eager, positive response — he can tell the prophets are in the pay of King Ahab and that they will say whatever Ahab wants them to say. Micaiah ben Imlah is called, against Ahab's desires, and tells the kings that the false prophets all have lying spirits in them. Zedekiah, the leader of the false prophets, asks a rhetorical question of Micaiah that assumes he himself has the Spirit of the Lord and Micaiah does not. This question indicates that both men, and presumably the rest of the court, believe that the Spirit of the Lord is in the true prophets, while he is not in false prophets. The issue is how to discern the identity of the true and false prophets.

Micaiah warns that Zedekiah will see by the historical results: Will Ahab be victorious, as Zedekiah prophesies, or will he lose to the Syrians, as Micaiah prophesies? This criterion is based on Deuteronomy 18:22: "When a prophet speaks in the name of the Lord, if the word does not come to pass or come true, that is a word which the Lord has not spoken; the prophet has spoken it presumptuously, you need not be afraid of him."

Of course, Micaiah spoke the true prophecy: the battle was lost, and both kings were mortally wounded and died (1 Kings 22:29-40). Micaiah was the true prophet with the Spirit of the Lord.

STUDY

Elisha

In our next passages, Elisha receives the Spirit of Elijah. When Elijah was at Mount Horeb (the northern dialect name for Sinai), listening to the Lord speak in a "still small voice" (1 Kings 19:12), the Lord instructed him to choose Elisha as his successor. As the end of Elijah's ministry approaches, the two prophets cross the Jordan.

 Stop here and read **2 Kings 2:9-18** in your own Bible.

While the term "Spirit of the Lord" is not used, Elisha does make a request to "inherit a double share of your spirit" (2 Kings 2:9). This refers to being a "man of God," a term used for Moses, Elijah, and Elisha because they were prophets who not only spoke God's word but also were used to perform miracles. This was distinct from prophets who primarily spoke God's words without miracles. On the assumption that the "spirit of Elijah" (2 Kings 2:15) is God's Spirit, making it possible to speak God's word and do miracles, Elisha picks up Elijah's mantle, strikes the Jordan River with it, and says, "Where is the LORD, the God of Elijah?" (2 Kings 2:14). At that moment, the water parts, and Elisha crosses the river without getting wet.

Speaking the word and seeing the miracle was proof that God had given Elisha "the spirit of Elijah," making Elisha a man of God like Elijah. He would continue to prophesy and do miracles until his death, and even afterward.

BONES OF SAINTS

2 Kings 13:20-21 is the text lying behind the use of the bones of saints as relics to bring healing:

> So Elisha died, and they buried him. Now bands of Moabites used to invade the land in the spring of the year. And as a man was being buried, behold, a marauding band was seen and the man was cast into the grave of Elisha; and as soon as the man touched the bones of Elisha, he revived, and stood on his feet. (RSV-SCE)

CONSIDER

The Chronicler

While the Books of Joshua, Judges, Samuel, and Kings tell the history of Israel from the perspective of the Book of Deuteronomy and is called the "Deuteronomistic History," the "Chronicler" is a school that wrote the Books of Chronicles, Ezra, and Nehemiah from the perspective of the theology of the priests writing after the return from exile in Babylon. Often the Chronicler includes stories directly from the Deuteronomistic History, but also contains many episodes that are not found there, apparently using sources that were not available to the Deuteronomistic historians. This section of our study will include three episodes that speak of the Spirit of God with the prophets.

Stop here and read **2 Chronicles 15:1-7** in your own Bible.

The first text speaks of an otherwise unknown prophet named Azariah the son of Oded, who prophesied during the reign of King Asa of Judah (913-873 B.C.). The event behind his prophecy was

47

an attempt by Pharaoh Osorkon in 899 B.C. to assert control over Judah with an invading army led by the Ethiopian general Zerah. The prophet Azariah experiences the "Spirit of God" coming upon him, and he summons King Asa and all the people to listen to his words of promise that the Lord is with them. Yet they still have a basic choice: to seek and find him or to forsake him and be forsaken by him. Azariah calls them to have courage and promises them reward for their work.

His prophecy was a success. The king and people listened, found courage, and removed all idols, including those belonging to Asa's own mother. In this, the nation purified its faith in the Lord, and there was peace throughout the rest of Asa's long reign as king of Judah.

 Stop here and read **2 Chronicles 20:14-30** in your own Bible.

In the second text, the "Spirit of the LORD" also comes upon the prophet Jahaziel the son of Zechariah, a Levite of the Asaph clan. The family of Asaph is well known from a number of psalms composed by clan members (Psalms 50, 73-83) as well as important priests of the same clan. Here the Spirit of the Lord strengthens Jahaziel to prophesy to King Jehoshaphat (r. 873-853 B.C.), the son of King Asa, and to the people of Judah at a time when the Moabites, Ammonites, and Meunites are marching to attack Judah. He tells the king and people not to fear because the Lord, not they, will defeat the enemy. This prophecy comes true as the Levites and the king rouse the people to praise God and have courage. The invading armies begin to kill one another before meeting the army of Judah, and the nation is spared.

 Stop here and read **2 Chronicles 24:20-22** in your own Bible.

The third episode is tragic. The Spirit of God "clothed" (literal Hebrew for "took possession of") the prophet Zechariah the son of Jehoiada the priest (2 Chron 24:20). However, his words are accusatory to King Joash (r. 835-797 B.C.), who, as an eight-year-old prince, had been saved from murder by his nurse, Jehosheba, and her husband, the high priest, Jehoiada. Zechariah is the son of Jehosheba and Jehoiada, so he feels confident to speak plainly to the king about breaking the Lord's commandments and thereby being forsaken by the Lord! Joash does not take the criticism well, so he murders Zechariah. As he is dying, Zechariah prays that the Lord avenge the murder, which he does when King Joash is assassinated in 797 B.C.

STUDY

So far we have examined the Spirit of the Lord God working through those prophets whose stories are told in various historical books, such as Numbers, the Deuteronomistic History, and the Chronicler. There are other prophets who wrote their own books, either themselves or with the help of scribes (e.g., Baruch was Jeremiah's scribe). Their writing styles vary; Isaiah and Amos are rather sophisticated in style, but Micah is not. The Hebrew dialect also varies; Hosea displays a northern dialect of Hebrew, Isaiah a southern dialect, and Jeremiah is a mixture, since he came from Anathoth, a town near the border of Israel and Judah. Yet each prophet speaks God's word to his own time and place. Many of them mention the role of the Spirit in their writings, some more and others not at all. We will examine their understanding of the role of the Spirit in their prophecies chronologically.

Hosea

The first prophet to mention the Holy Spirit is Hosea, who began his prophesying in the 740s B.C. and continued into the late 720s at least. This was a period in which the northern Kingdom of Israel went from its high point of wealth and power to its complete destruction by the Assyrians.

The part of Hosea we are concerned with was composed when Hosea criticized Israel for trusting in Assyria instead of the Lord. More specifically, Hosea 9:1-9 was delivered to the people during the New Year and harvest festivals in the autumn, as a criticism of the false prophets of the time.

 Stop here and read **Hosea 5:8-9:9** in your own Bible.

From this message we can derive that the prophets had been preaching success and prosperity as the upcoming promise of the new king, Hoshea. For his part, the prophet Hosea announces that the day of recompense or payback will be punishment because of the many sins and the people's lack of trust in the Lord. Because the false prophets announced good news, Hosea calls them fools and crazy, even though they are men "of the spirit" (Hos 9:7). Having a reputation for possessing the Spirit of the Lord does not guarantee ongoing faithfulness to him. The prophets who have the Spirit of the Lord must constantly discern what the Lord is saying and not use their past experience to sway their views of the present or to cease being attentive and obedient to God.

Micah

Micah came from western Judah and was a man of the country-side, in distinction to his contemporary Isaiah, who was a sophisticated urban dweller in Jerusalem. Both Micah and Isaiah were contemporaries of the northern prophet, Hosea, and they also struggled in this difficult period of Assyrian takeover of western Asia by Tiglath-Pileser III.

Micah speaks twice of the Spirit of the Lord and the prophets, in the same way as Hosea: false prophets try to prevent him from giving his message, but he corrects them.

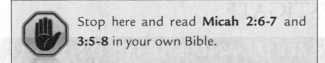

Stop here and read **Micah 2:6-7** and **3:5-8** in your own Bible.

Micah rhetorically asks the false prophets who are trying to prevent him from speaking his warnings against the people: "Should this be said?" (Mic 2:7). The implied answer is, "No, it should not be said." Then he rhetorically asks if their actions come from the Spirit of the Lord, and the implied answer is that they do not. Rather, the words of the Lord, which come from his Spirit, will do good to people — but only if they are upright. The false prophets and the rest of their listeners are, by implication, not upright, so Micah's warnings will do them no good.

Like others, Micah experienced significant opposition from false prophets. These were prophets who responded to bribes: pay them something and they say favorable things; give them nothing and receive their condemnation. He then lays out their punishment: God will give them no answer, no matter what methods of divining the future they may try. On the other hand, Micah announces that he is filled with power — the Spirit of the Lord. He does not derive power from any gifts other humans might bestow but from the Spirit of the Lord. Along with this power comes justice and "might" — that is, the kind of power that a warrior might have. With these qualities from the Spirit of the Lord, Micah is able to declare the "transgression" — that is, the rebelliousness and sins of the people (Mic 3:8).

Ezekiel

The prophet Ezekiel was a priest who was taken into exile in Babylon in 598 B.C., the first time Nebuchadnezzar (also spelled Nebuchadrezzar in thirty-three verses in Jeremiah and Ezekiel) subjected Judah and took 10,000 people, especially the leaders, captive into Babylon. He experienced a number of visions and other powerful experiences of the Lord, frequently describing how the Lord's Spirit empowered him to prophesy.

INVESTIGATE

EZEKIEL AND THE LORD'S SPIRIT

 Look up the following passages and make notes on Ezekiel's visions and any mention of the Lord's Spirit.

PASSAGE	NOTES
Ezekiel 1	
Ezekiel 2:1-2	
Ezekiel 2:3-8	
Ezekiel 3:11-17	
Ezekiel 3:22-27	

52

Stop here and read **Ezekiel 43:4-5** in your own Bible.

At this point, the glory of the Lord returns to the Temple. This glory left the Temple because of the sins of the people; now the glory returns. Just as the Spirit had lifted him up to witness the people's sins and the Lord's departure, so now the Spirit returns him to the Temple to witness the return of the glory of the Lord as it fills the Temple.

Zechariah

Zechariah began his prophecies in October of 520 B.C., when the people were inspired by the prophet Haggai to start rebuilding the Temple, and he continued until the Temple was finished. He understood that the nation's identity came from the Lord, so the Temple was a key component of the post-exilic restoration.

Stop here and read **Zechariah 6:6-8** in your own Bible.

The first mention of the Spirit occurs in a vision of four chariots that patrol the four directions on the earth. "The chariot with the black horses goes toward the north country" (Zech 6:6), the direction from which invaders had come, whether Assyrians or Babylonians. In contrast, the Lord's Spirit finds rest in the north. This unexpected peace from the north comes because the angel in that chariot in the north finds a number of men among the exiles who have silver and gold for making a crown for the high priest, Joshua son of Jehoza-dak, the high priest. To him he announces that a man called "the Branch" will rebuild the Temple (Zech 6:12). Such a promise of hope for the Temple, the high priest, and the political leader is what gives the Spirit rest in the north.

 Stop here and read **Zechariah 7:9-14** in your own Bible.

In 518 B.C., Zechariah speaks this oracle to a group of men who have come to Jerusalem to ask a question about continuing a fast they have been doing. At this point, Zechariah speaks of the Lord's words to Israel in the past, especially concerning his pro-phetic exhortations of past centuries, calling the people to do right, show mercy, and avoid evil. However, Zechariah points out that the ancestors refused to listen to the Lord's law and words that he "had sent by his Spirit" (Zech 7:12). This verse identifies the words of the Law and the prophets — the whole of the Old Testament — as hav-ing been spoken by the Lord's Spirit. This prepares the way for the important claim of the Nicene Creed that is recited on Sundays and solemnities: "He [the Holy Spirit] has spoken through the prophets."

THE INSPIRATION OF THE HOLY SPIRIT

The Church has cherished the Old Testament as God's word from the time of the New Testament writers (360 quotes of the Old Testament are in the New), through the Councils of Nicaea, Florence, Trent, and Vatican II. The New Testament agrees with Zechariah's point that the Holy Spirit inspired the Old Testament books. For instance, Matthew 22:43 attributes David's authorship of Psalm 110 to the inspiration of the Holy Spirit. These claims became important when Gnostic groups and others, such as Marcion, rejected the inspira-tion, truth, and role of the Old Testament in Scripture.

STUDY

Isaiah

The Book of Isaiah is a collection of prophecies from different periods of Israel's history, as indicated by the references to present events from different periods. The last segment (Isaiah 56-66) is identified as Trito-Isaiah, an unnamed prophet who understood that his ministry was made possible by the Spirit of the Lord.

Trito-Isaiah wrote at the time after the returned Jewish exiles had rebuilt the Temple in Jerusalem, perhaps a generation after Haggai and Zechariah had successfully stirred the people to rebuild it between 520 and 516 B.C. However, life in Jerusalem was not as ideal as Haggai and Zechariah had promised. Some people had become quite wealthy while others remained poor. Isaiah 59:1-20 describes the injustice in court that the poor were commonly experiencing, and through the prophet the Lord decries this as a breach of the covenant he had made with the people. The Lord promises to judge the wicked for their deeds and redeem those who repent. Then he addresses the prophet Trito-Isaiah.

Stop here and read **Isaiah 59:21** in your own Bible.

The Lord begins by reaffirming that he is maintaining a covenant with the people, which takes the form of placing his Spirit on the prophet so as to give him the Lord's words. He promises that these words will continue in his descendants for generations, as the evidence of the reading of this book of the Bible for about 2,500 years indicates. The Spirit of the Lord gives words of lasting value, and they still form the way people think. Not only has this prophecy of the long-lasting authority of the word of the Lord through his Spirit come true, but also this is a model by which all of Scripture has been understood. This passage would have influenced Paul's teaching that "all scripture is inspired by God" (2 Tim 3:16).

Stop here and read Isaiah **61:1-3** in your own Bible.

This passage that "proclaim[s] the year of the LORD's favor" (Is 61:2) is a reference to the Jubilee Year, probably the first Jubilee after the Temple was finished in 516 B.C., therefore dating this to 473 B.C., 100 years after Ezekiel's Jubilee prophecy of the restored Temple in Ezekiel 40-48. Trito-Isaiah's Jerusalem continues to experience the oppression of the poor by the wealthy, so he receives the anointing by "Spirit of the Lord GOD" (Is 61:1) in order to announce hope to the poor, who mourn in Zion of his day.

CONSIDER

Sirach

Sirach wrote his book of wisdom in the 190s B.C.

Stop here and read **Sirach 48:22-25** in your own Bible.

Toward the end of his book, he gives a wisdom perspective on the ancient heroes of Israel. Among these heroes are King Hezekiah, one of the few good kings, and the prophet Isaiah, who prophesied throughout the reigns of Hezekiah's grandfather, father, Hezekiah's own reign, and into that of Hezekiah's wicked son, Manasseh. Sirach states that Isaiah saw the last things to come in the future and hidden mysteries — all "by the spirit of might" (Sir 48:24). This indicates that into the later years of Israel's history, and even in the wisdom tradition, which depended more on experience and reason than direct inspiration, the power of the Holy Spirit was understood to lie behind Isaiah, and indeed all of the prophets.

DISCUSS

1. List some of the ways that the Spirit of God made himself known through the prophets.
2. What is one new idea or insight about the Lord's Spirit that you have gained from this chapter?
3. Do you think the Holy Spirit speaks through people today? Why or why not?

PRACTICE

This week, choose one of the prophets from the Old Testament and read his prophecies. Use his words of encouragement, warning, hope, and call to repentance as a guide for your own life.

Session 4

GIVER OF WISDOM, GUIDANCE, AND TRUTH

> "Remember, then, that you received a spiritual seal, *the spirit of wisdom and understanding, the spirit of knowledge and reverence, the spirit of holy fear.* Keep safe what you received. God the Father sealed you, Christ the Lord strengthened you and sent the Spirit into your hearts as the pledge of what is to come."
>
> — ST. AMBROSE, *On the Mysteries* (*The Liturgy of the Hours*, emphasis in the original)

Wisdom is a major stream of biblical tradition, appearing in books such as Proverbs, Sirach, the Wisdom of Solomon, Job, and Ecclesiastes. The Psalter includes a number of wisdom psalms; prophets, like Amos, use wisdom forms of speech and images; and Deuteronomy includes strains of thought from wisdom in its considerations of the Law and history.

The main characteristics of wisdom are experience, reflection on that experience, and conclusions drawn by reason from experience and reflection. These elements of wisdom do not lend themselves so strongly to the divine inspiration usually associated with Moses the lawgiver, the prophets, King David, or the biblical historians. However, the wisdom books frequently state the theme that "The fear of the LORD is the beginning of wisdom" (Prov 9:10), showing an element of faith as the basis of wisdom. Wisdom is often personified as a lady who has great power to help a person if her closeness with God and store of knowledge is trusted (Prov 8-9). In this session, we will examine passages that explicitly link wisdom and various skills to the Spirit of the Lord God.

STUDY

Practical wisdom refers to the type of know-how associated with the practical tasks of living in the world well. Most of the time, the practical details of life flow from experience and knowledge of certain skills and tasks, such as pottery, metal working, carpentry, cooking, and so on. However, in some extraordinary cases, these practical gifts are recognized as gifts of God's Spirit.

Skills and Crafts

Bezalel was not merely a clever craftsman, but the Lord had "filled him with the Spirit of God, with ability and intelligence, with knowledge and all craftsmanship" (Ex 31:3, 35:31). His human skill was not rejected or denied, but the Spirit of God brought it up to a new level. This was especially important since he was getting a description of the Tent of Meeting, the Ark of the Covenant, and the altars and utensils as Moses received the messages from God. The Spirit of God was needed so that he could transform Moses' descriptions into actuality.

INVESTIGATE

THE GIFTS OF LIFE

The Bible shows great appreciation for these gifts in different areas of life, as the following passages indicate. Look up the following passages and make notes on the crafts involved and any mention of the Spirit of God.

PASSAGE	NOTES
Exodus 31:2-5	

Exodus 35:30-33	
Exodus 36:1-2	

Dream Interpretation

Ancient people frequently sought to know the future, frequently using magical means of fortune-telling, consulting dead spirits, and astrology. In many Scripture passages, Israel was forbidden to practice such magic. However, a few passages recognized that God could speak through dreams, and in two of them (both regarding the dreams of foreign kings) the Spirit of God is credited with the power given to interpret them.

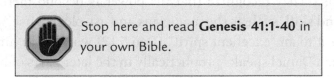

Stop here and read **Genesis 41:1-40** in your own Bible.

The story of Joseph and his brothers begins in Genesis 37, 39-41, covering Joseph being sold into slavery in Egypt and his rise to power before a seven-year famine. The key to his success is a God-given ability to interpret dreams. Having done so for Pharaoh, he advises a strategy of organizing the surplus of the seven good years so as to prepare for the seven lean years. At that point, Pharaoh enthusiastically recognizes Joseph's God-given abilities.

Pharaoh recognizes that the Spirit of God dwells in Joseph in an exceptional way. Therefore, that qualifies him to be second-in-command in Egypt. The gift of the Spirit makes him an extraordinarily good administrator. (We will see that administrators are among the gifts of the Holy Spirit in 1 Corinthians 12:28.)

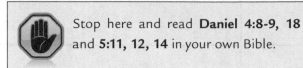

Stop here and read **Daniel 4:8-9, 18** and **5:11, 12, 14** in your own Bible.

Daniel was taken into exile in Babylon in 598 B.C. While living there, he and three companions were chosen to serve the king, and he acquired a reputation for great wisdom and knowledge, especially in dream interpretation. In Daniel 4, King Nebuchadnezzar asks him to interpret a dream, but he understands Daniel's powers through the lens of a Chaldean pagan who worships many gods and uses magicians to understand them. For that reason, he calls Daniel by his Babylonian name, Belteshazzar, and he considers Daniel "the chief of the magicians" (Dan 4:9). He also believes that "the spirit of the holy gods" (Dan 4:9) is working through Daniel, giving him the ability to interpret dreams.

On these occasions when Daniel interprets dreams for the kings of Babylon, they understand that he is acting by the "spirit of the holy gods." They recognize that the power is beyond mere human ability and skill, such as the magicians and astrologers use, and they attribute it to an "excellent spirit" (Dan 5:12) working in him. However, when Daniel speaks prophetically in the later parts of his book, this phrase does not appear. His inspiration by God is assumed in the passages concerned with the prophecies regarding Israel.

CONSIDER

Another area of practical wisdom is political leadership, widely defined to include tribal, royal, and judicial abilities. Many skills are needed by leaders — the ability to inspire others, to lead them in battle, to judge legal cases, and to run an administration. These skills require wisdom and virtue, for which reason the Spirit of the

Lord God works to raise up and direct leaders, kings, and judges in Israel.

Moses' Helpers

Moses was overwhelmed by the complaints of the people and the tasks of leadership in Israel, so the Lord offered him help by calling for seventy men to receive a portion of the Spirit that he had placed upon Moses. These leaders would help "bear the burden of the people" (Num 11:17).

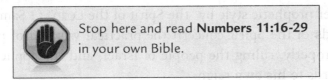

Stop here and read **Numbers 11:16-29** in your own Bible.

An intriguing part of the Lord's instructions in this passage is his statement, "I will take some of the spirit which is upon you and put it upon them" (Num 11:17). No text states this at an earlier stage, that the Lord had given Moses his Spirit, but this passage assumes that Moses has acted so far under the guidance of God's Spirit and that this same Spirit can be given to other people by God. Moses himself does not have control of this Spirit. Furthermore, by receiving a portion of God's Spirit, the seventy leaders will be able to exercise a portion of the leadership of the people beyond their natural gifts of leadership, since all of them already have had some position of authority either by their birth-given status or by exercising certain abilities of leadership. Those natural gifts were insufficient for the burden of leading the former slaves to the Promised Land, so God bestows his Spirit to enable them to do much more.

The next stage in this narrative depicts the Lord's descent in a cloud to speak with Moses, as on other occasions, and to bestow the portions of the Spirit upon the seventy elders, including two who remained in the camp. (Later, at the Transfiguration, the surrounding cloud would also be an external sign of the presence of the Holy Spirit.) These men begin to prophesy, probably a reference to the type of ecstatic prophecy experienced by the bands of prophets and

Saul. This is a onetime experience that Moses wishes would affect the whole nation, but it does not. That general experience of the Holy Spirit among the people will not take place until Pentecost and beyond. This passage also demonstrates that the Spirit is under the Lord's control, as seen in his gift to Eldad and Medad, who receive it in the camp and not in the separate place outside the camp with the other sixty-eight men.

The Lord's Last Words to David

David, the "sweet psalmist of Israel," received his "last words" in a rather prophetic style by "the Spirit of the LORD" (2 Sam 23:1-2). The words of the Spirit concern the practical wisdom of properly, and improperly, ruling the people of Israel, and the application of these words to his own reign.

 Stop here and read **2 Samuel 23:1-7** in your own Bible.

David opens the oracle with a statement of principles that the "God of Israel" teaches that a just king rules "in the fear of God" (2 Sam 23:3), knowing that a power far greater than he will call him to account for his righteous or unrighteous ways. The effects of a just ruler on the people are compared to the morning light and the rain that bring growth from the earth. David applies this to his own house or reign. He cites "the everlasting covenant" (2 Sam 23:5) the Lord made that his descendant would reign forever, as well as the practical results in the order and security during his reign. In conclusion, he compares the "godless" — that is, "worthless" people (2 Sam 23:6) — to useless thorns that cannot even be touched with the hand but are picked up with a spear in order to throw them into a fire.

David wants his reign and that of other kings to be evaluated by these norms given by the "Spirit of the Lord." Power itself is insufficient; justice and fear of the Lord are the ultimate norms.

STUDY

Hope for the Messiah

The Lord promises to destroy the great Assyrian Empire in Isaiah 10, with hope for Jerusalem to be saved and a remnant of people to survive. The Lord's protection of Jerusalem was a great theme in Proto-Isaiah, despite Israel's sins and failings.

Isaiah 11 takes up another great theme of salvation: the renewal of the Davidic kingship. Hope is hinted at in the sign of the virgin giving birth to Immanuel in Isaiah 7:14; more explicit hope for the newborn son of David's line is expressed after the Assyrian defeat of the Northern Kingdom. Here, Isaiah 11:1-9 and 11:10-16 speak of a much fuller hope for the Davidic Messiah.

>
> Stop here and read **Isaiah 11:1-16** in your own Bible.

This messianic prophecy opens with both hope and disappointment. Jesse was David's father and therefore is the root of David's line. However, the Davidic kings were disappointments, with some few exceptions like Jehoshaphat, Hezekiah, and Josiah. Therefore, the Davidic family tree will be cut down, leaving only a "stump of Jesse" (Is 11:1) (David's name is not used because his descendants were so bad), from which a new shoot will come.

NEW SHOOTS

Olive tree stumps often have new shoots that grow into new branches as large as the original trunk. The Hebrew word for "shoot" is *netzer*, which is the root of the name "Nazareth," and it explains why Matthew 2:23 says Jesus will be called a "Nazarene," since he is the shoot that fulfills Isaiah 11:1.

Recall that when the prophet Samuel anointed David as king to replace Saul, "the spirit of the LORD came mightily upon" him (1 Sam 16:13-14). Now Isaiah prophesies that the Messiah will be filled with the same Spirit of the Lord. The Spirit will fill the Messiah with wisdom, understanding, counsel, might, knowledge, and fear of the Lord — virtues that humans can learn, but not with the same power as the Spirit of the Lord can bestow. The Spirit will enable the Messiah to exercise the royal power of judging people, but not by externals. He will be committed only to justice and righteousness, such as God can do, but which should characterize people as well.

The poor and the meek will benefit from the Messiah's authentic equity, but he will know and punish the wicked "with the rod of his mouth and his breath" (see Rev 1:16, 2:16; 19:15). The Messiah will wear righteousness and faithfulness as his girdle, wrapping the lower part of the trunk of the body, where are found the kidneys and intestines, the organs in which the free will and decision making are located, according to Hebrew understanding of the human person.

Recall that Isaiah 40-55 was written around 540 B.C. or slightly earlier, as the Persians led by King Cyrus the Great began the process of defeating the Babylonian Empire, which led to the release of the Jews from exile.

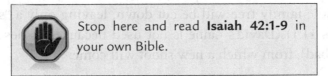
Stop here and read **Isaiah 42:1-9** in your own Bible.

The Church understands this as a prophecy of Jesus the Messiah. This first "Song of the Servant of the Lord" is the only one that mentions the Lord's Spirit. Isaiah 45:1 identifies Cyrus, the king of the Persians, as the one "whose right hand I have grasped, / to subdue nations before him." Isaiah 42:1-9 does not mention Cyrus by name but is speaking of him as the one who will establish justice on earth at that time. For our study, he is yet another king, though a foreign one, whom the Spirit of the Lord leads in doing what is right. As such, he is a foreign example of David's last words about kingship and just rule and the ideal of the future Messiah from David's lineage.

It is also important to note that the absence of Cyrus' name in this servant song made it easy to apply the prophecy to Jesus Christ on at least three occasions: the Father speaking at Jesus' baptism and transfiguration, as well as in a summary of Jesus' healing ministry in Matthew 12:17-20.

CONSIDER

Susanna

The story of Susanna (Daniel 13) concerns a beautiful Jewish woman living in the Babylonian exile who refuses to be seduced by two Jewish elders. They falsely accuse her of adultery with some young man, and people are about to stone her to death. However, God stirs up "the holy spirit" in the young boy Daniel to stop the crowd. He then cross-examines the two elders as to the type of tree they found her near, and they each say a different kind, neither of which can be mistaken for the other.

The Holy Spirit thereby prevented the unjust punishment of Susanna, and the two elders were executed for bearing false witness against her. Through all this, correct judgment of a legal case was made possible by the Spirit.

STUDY

The Book of Wisdom was written in Greek in Alexandria, Egypt, by a Jew trying to show the superiority of biblical wisdom over Greek philosophy. At times, he speaks as if he were a king seeking wisdom, and twice he recognizes that the Spirit of wisdom is superior to wealth and power. This Spirit of wisdom comes from God, so he prays for it, knowing that he cannot produce such wisdom on his own power or intellect. This certainly is parallel to the way Jesus speaks of the "Spirit of truth" in John 14-16, except for the fact that here the king can merely petition God for the Spirit; Jesus will petition the Father and bestow the Spirit of truth.

INVESTIGATE

BIBLICAL WISDOM

 Look up the following passages and make notes on the Spirit of wisdom.

PASSAGE	NOTES
Wisdom 7:7-9	
Wisdom 9:17-18	

STUDY

We have looked at the way the Spirit of the Lord God helped leaders at the various stages of Israel's development. In addition to the leaders, judges, and kings, the rest of the people sought God's guidance through many different kinds of situations. A number of passages attribute God's help to his Spirit.

We begin this section about the leading of the Spirit of God with a psalm.

 Stop here and read **Psalm 143** in your own Bible.

The Psalms belonged to the whole people, who prayed them in the Temple together or as individuals. Psalm 143 is a lament of an individual whose sin results in enemies attacking him. In the face of this attack, his own "spirit faints," and his heart "is appalled" (Ps 143:4). Since he cannot depend on his own weak spirit and heart, he seeks help from God. He professes his faith that God's Spirit is good, therefore he asks for his guidance. Before that request he first asks the Lord to "teach me to do your will" (Ps 143:10) as a prerequisite for allowing the Spirit to lead him. The good Spirit cannot truly guide a person who does not want to do the will of God.

The Spirit and the People

Earlier, we saw that Ezekiel's own prophetic ministry was made possible only by the Spirit of the Lord. However, twice he recognized that the whole people need the Spirit of the Lord in order to live out the covenant as the Lord required of them.

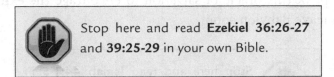

Stop here and read **Ezekiel 36:26-27** and **39:25-29** in your own Bible.

Although Ezekiel accuses the people living with him in exile in Babylon of having hearts of stone that are incapable of authentic love, he does not leave them in despair. Rather, Ezekiel receives a prophecy from the Lord that he will bestow new hearts of flesh to replace their stone-cold hearts, and then he will bestow his Spirit upon them.

The Lord's Spirit will be effective within them because of their new hearts of flesh. His Spirit cannot operate in hearts of stone, but only within that which is authentically human. This is an important assertion that human beings were created to be capable of receiving God's activity within them. Yet this is possible only when they are most human. Sometimes people identify being human with being a fallen sinner, and there is a truth to that. However, when God looks at the meaning of true and authentic humanity, he sees the capacity to receive his own Spirit. That Spirit will enable and empower the human hearts to obey his laws, because in his mind, being good and holy is true humanity.

Here the Lord explains again that he sent the Israelites into exile because of their many sins — a point made repeatedly by both Jeremiah and Ezekiel before the exile took place. However, he also promises to bring all his people back to the Promised Land. At that point, the Lord will let them see his face, but only after he pours out his Spirit (Ezek 39:29). This is a promise of the universal outpouring of the Holy Spirit on Pentecost.

CONSIDER

The exiled Jews heard Deutero-Isaiah's initial prophecies that the Lord was about to set them free from exile in Babylon, but apparently many of them did not believe it. At this point, the Lord inspires him to speak this oracle of salvation to encourage the exiles to be ready to leave Babylon soon.

 Stop here and read **Isaiah 44:1-5** in your own Bible.

After urging Jacob, the Lord's servant, to "hear" his word, the Lord orders the people to "Fear not," and he then identifies Jacob/Jeshurun as the Lord's "chosen" (Is 44:1, 2). Jeshurun is a name for Israel found only in poetic texts, from the root *jashar*, meaning to be "upright."

Then the Lord proclaims that salvation will occur in a future when he transforms both the land and the people. While the dry land will be transformed by the outpouring of water, Israel's descendants will be transformed by the outpouring of the Lord's Spirit. Only by the outpouring of the Lord's Spirit like rain will they be able to identify themselves as truly belonging to the Lord. This will have an impact on Paul's teaching that Christians will be able to identify

Jesus as Lord (1 Cor 12:3) and God as their Father (Rom 8:15; Gal 4:6) only by the power of the Holy Spirit. The Lord's Spirit guides people into their truest identity in God.

Stop here and read **Isaiah 48:12-17** in your own Bible.

These verses are a trial speech with Israel, which is summoned to listen to the Lord, the creator of everything, the beginning and end of all existence. The Lord arraigns the false gods of Babylon so as to induce Israel to draw close to the Lord and listen to him with trust, to know that he is truly the beginning and the end who knows the best way for them to follow. Deutero-Isaiah here continues to sever Israel's connections with the Babylonian gods and culture. In Isaiah 48:16, the Lord tells Israel to draw near to understand that the Lord's words govern salvation history, just as he created everything simply by his word. At this moment of Israel's exile in Babylon, when the Lord seems too weak to help and the people have given up hope, the Lord has sent Deutero-Isaiah and his own Spirit in order to set them free.

The Jewish people began returning from Babylon in 538 B.C., just three months after Cyrus the Persian conquered Babylon and set them free. The returnees started to rebuild the Temple but stopped after the foundation was laid, and they began building their own homes first. In August/September of 520 B.C., the prophet Haggai called the people to finish building the Temple, and they began building again in late September or October. At that point, Haggai prophesied to the governor Zerubbabel and the high priest Joshua, saying that the Lord was with their efforts.

Stop here and read **Haggai 2:4-7** in your own Bible.

These efforts to build the Temple are possible because the Lord's own Spirit dwells among the people. On that basis, they need not fear. The same Spirit who guided Bezalel to craft the original tent and its vessels will strengthen and guide the leaders and people to rebuild the ruined Temple. In addition, the Lord will "shake the heavens and the earth and the sea" (Hag 2:6) to bring the riches of the nation to rebuild the Temple with splendor. This passage will later influence Paul, who wrote of the human body as the Temple of the Spirit and the whole Church as the Temple of the Holy Spirit.

Zechariah also begins to prophesy at about the same time as Haggai, with the same message. He, like Haggai, reminds the people who are still rebuilding the Temple that neither their might nor their power is sufficient to complete the task. The Lord's Spirit is necessary: "Then he said to me, 'This is the word of the LORD to Zerubbabel: Not by might, nor by power, but by my Spirit, says the LORD of hosts'" (Zech 4:6).

Dating the Book of Joel is impossible, but most scholars place it some years after the return from the exile. The important fact is the plague of locusts that hits the country, which is the occasion for Joel to call for the people to repent, pray, and fast. When the people heed his warning, the Lord pities them and grants them a good crop and promises to remain in their midst. After accepting their repentance, the Lord also makes a promise to send his Spirit upon the whole people.

Stop here and read **Joel 2:28-31** in your own Bible.

Just as Moses expressed a wish that the whole nation would receive the Spirit of God and prophesy, now the prophet Joel prophesies that the Lord will indeed pour out his Spirit on all flesh — young and old, master and servant, male and female. As seen in Peter's sermon in Acts 2:14-36, this prophecy would be fulfilled on Pentecost.

STUDY

The Holy Spirit and Repentance

The process of repentance of sin is never easy for people: sometimes they enjoy their sins; sometimes they are too proud to humble themselves in repentance; sometimes they are so terrified of God that they fear they can never be forgiven. For that reason, they need help within their hearts and souls to be able to repent, and the Israelites learned that the Spirit of the Lord could and would help them.

> Stop here and read **Psalm 51** in your own Bible.

This is the greatest of the penitential psalms, expressing repentance in a profound prayer that describes the feelings of repentant sinners throughout the ages. After having confessed his sins in the preceding verses, David wants the sin replaced with "a clean heart" and a "new and right spirit" that is a "willing spirit" (Ps 51:10, 12). To make this possible, he asks that God's Holy Spirit remain with him, because such newness is not possible without the Holy Spirit of God.

RUAH

Ruah, the word for "spirit," is the same, whether referring to God's Holy Spirit or David's human spirit. It can be either masculine or feminine, as detected by the adjectives or verbs (both of which indicate gender in Hebrew and the other Semitic languages). In this passage, *ruah* is feminine when referring to the human spirit that is right and willing; *ruah* is masculine when referring to the Lord's Holy Spirit.

INVESTIGATE

THE SINS OF THE NATION

 Look up the following passages and make notes on the sins of the nation and the Lord's judgment.

PASSAGE	NOTES
Isaiah 2:6-22	
Isaiah 3:1-11	
Isaiah 3:12-15	
Isaiah 3:16-4:1	
Isaiah 4:2-6	

Jerusalem's survivors will be holy and "recorded for life" (Is 4:3) in the Lord's book, like registered citizens. These holy survivors will have their stain of sin "washed away" with the Lord's "spirit of judgment" and "burning" (Is 4:4). This prophecy relates to John the Baptist's saying that Christ would baptize people "with the Holy Spirit and with fire" (Mt 3:11). It also helps our understanding of Christ's words, that "unless one is born of water and the Spirit, he cannot enter the kingdom of God" (Jn 3:5).

 Stop here and read **Isaiah 30:1-5** in your own Bible.

These verses are a proclamation of woe against King Hezekiah of Judah, who rebelled against God by making an alliance with Egyptian Pharaoh Shebitku's rebellion against King Sennacherib of Assyria. Isaiah warns Hezekiah that trust in the pharaoh will lead to humiliation, which indeed happened. Pharaoh Shebitku sends his son Tirhakah (Taharqa) with an army that is defeated in the open field, and Tirhakah takes refuge in Lachish, a Judahite city southwest of Jerusalem. Sennacherib attacks Lachish and destroys it.

The key to the "sin" mentioned in Isaiah 30:1 is that King Hezekiah's plans were not from the Lord's Spirit. Isaiah believes that the Spirit of the Lord can and should guide the nation. If the people of Judah would heed the Lord, as he speaks through Isaiah, Lachish and other cities would not be devastated.

 Stop here and read **Isaiah 32:15-20** in your own Bible.

This selection is a description of salvation that looks beyond the present distress to a transformation of the land accomplished by the Spirit of the Lord. It recognizes that the Spirit of the Lord is the necessary gift that precedes the return to abundant crops, even in the wilderness. Just as the Spirit that fills the Messiah led to a transformation of all the earth and its animals, so here the Spirit will transform the desert and forest into places of abundant crops. The Spirit will effect justice and righteousness to bring about peace, quiet, and trust among the inhabitants of the land after the Assyrian army has departed.

CONSIDER

In the summer of 458 B.C., Ezra the priest and some companions came to Jerusalem to teach the people the Law of God. In 444 B.C., Nehemiah, a government official, came to assist Ezra and to help in rebuilding the walls of Jerusalem, which had been destroyed in 587 B.C., as a protection from marauders. The Jews had begun returning from Babylon in 539 B.C., almost a century earlier, and with the passage of years, they lost their fervor, so their faith needed revival even after the walls were rebuilt.

The dedication of the walls was celebrated first by a reading of the Law by Ezra and the priests, with the nobles and people gathered around on the feast of Rosh Hashanah — the New Year festival. Ten days later they celebrated the Day of Atonement, and on the twenty-fourth they fasted, read the Law for six hours, and then confessed their sins for another six hours. Ezra then led a prayer of repentance for all the nation's sins from the time of the Exodus forward and concluded with a renewal of the covenant with the Lord.

Stop here and read **Nehemiah 9:6-38** in your own Bible.

The Spirit of God in the Old Testament

The many passages considered in the Old Testament recognize that the Spirit of God bestows great power, extremely important gifts of prophetic truth and insight, as well as wisdom for all areas of life. The Bible does not deny that human nature has tremendous capacities to do great things, but the Spirit of the Lord God enables people to go far beyond their natural gifts.

Certainly the Old Testament does not define the Holy Spirit as the third Person of the Blessed Trinity, co-equal to the Father and Son in eternity, dignity, and divinity. Such clarity would be beyond the people and might even be confused with polytheism, the belief in multiple gods. The Old Testament focuses on accepting that God is one and that he is the only God who exists; the mystery of the Blessed Trinity would be revealed in Jesus' life and teaching. Yet, there are clues pointing to the Holy Spirit's divinity in the Old Testament. For instance, like God by his nature, the Spirit of God is everywhere, and a human cannot be in any place separate from him. Such omnipresence is not a quality of any creature but of God. Readers can rightly conclude that the omnipresent Spirit of the Lord is himself God.

Another divine quality of the Spirit of the Lord is his knowledge even of God's interior life. Repeatedly, various passages indicate the Spirit's knowledge of human hearts and minds. No one has directed the Spirit of the Lord or has enlightened him on justice, knowledge, or understanding. The Spirit of the Lord has all the power to direct himself, so he needs no one else. The implication is that the Spirit is also divine, though nothing more explicit is stated lest the ancients start thinking about the Spirit as an independent God, and there can be only one Lord.

Isaiah 57:14-21 states that the Spirit comes directly from the Lord God. Certainly these verses do not state that the Spirit is God, but it is absolutely clear that the Spirit comes directly from God. As later lessons will make clear, Jesus' teaching about the Holy Spirit in the Last Supper Discourse will show that the Holy Spirit of truth will be said to be sent both by God the Father and by the Son. The clue that points to Jesus' teaching can be found in the Old Testament, but it will need the clarity Jesus gives throughout his actions and teaching in regard to the Holy Spirit.

DISCUSS

1. This chapter looks at the Lord's Spirit as the giver of wisdom and truth. What are some of the examples of this that have impressed you?

2. At times, special creative gifts seem to come directly from the Spirit, as in the case of Bezalel, the craftsman (Ex 31:2). Think about some creative "geniuses" you might be familiar with. Do their abilities seem to come from the Spirit or their own talent?

3. Recall one or two Old Testament passages that point to the Holy Spirit as being God.

PRACTICE

The Holy Spirit is the source of wisdom and guidance in both the Old and the New Testaments. This week, before making any serious decisions, take time to pray to the Spirit for clarity and direction. Before you begin any creative endeavor, ask the Spirit for inspiration. Be sure to conclude your prayer with thanks!

Session 5

JESUS, THE HOLY SPIRIT, AND THE TRINITY

> "Paul, a servant of Jesus Christ, called to be an apostle, set apart for the gospel of God which he promised beforehand through his prophets in the holy scriptures, the gospel concerning his Son, who was descended from David according to the flesh and designated Son of God in power according to the Spirit of holiness by his resurrection from the dead, Jesus Christ our Lord."
>
> — ROMANS 1:1-4

The opening greeting to the Romans begins Paul's great epistle with a Trinitarian-based theology that permeates the whole New Testament. We begin our study of the Holy Spirit in the New Testament with the same desire to better understand the role of the Holy Spirit within the Blessed Trinity and within our own lives.

The Bible is not a theological treatise stating the logical principles of the Jewish and Christian religions. Rather, it is the history of the faith of a people in which various individuals and the community as a whole came to believe in one God, who cared for and directed their lives and history. For that reason we examine the various texts to help us better understand the identity and role of the Holy Spirit within the life and teaching of Jesus Christ. He, the Word of God made flesh, moves forward our understanding of the Holy Spirit beyond the early but very important clues about the Holy Spirit in the Old Testament to a greater fullness of knowing the Person of the Holy Spirit and his relationship with human beings.

STUDY

The Spirit and John the Baptist

The angel Gabriel appeared to Zechariah during his priestly ministry in the Temple, as he offered incense to the Lord. His message was the announcement of a son, John, later known as the Baptist.

 Stop here and read **Luke 1:13-17** in your own Bible.

The angel describes a number of John's characteristics, some of which are under Zechariah's control (the prohibition of wine and strong drink, which was a characteristic of the Nazirites); some are under the control of the people (they will rejoice at his birth); and still more that are under the control of the Lord God. The first of these is that he will be "filled with the Holy Spirit, even from his mother's womb" (Lk 1:15). This promise is along the line of Old Testament prophets that we saw in Session 2 of this study.

The second characteristic is that he will have the "spirit and power of Elijah" (Lk 1:17). This refers first of all to the story of Elijah's farewell to Elisha before his ascension in the fiery chariot in 2 Kings 2:9-12. In addition, the angel's words to Zechariah refer to the concluding prophecy of the Old Testament in Malachi: "Behold, I will send you Elijah the prophet before the great and terrible day of the LORD comes. And he will turn the hearts of fathers to their children and the hearts of children to their fathers, lest I come and smite the land with a curse" (Mal 4:5-6).

Not only does the angel Gabriel explicitly cite this prophecy, but Jesus later refers to John the Baptist as "Elijah."

INVESTIGATE

JOHN THE BAPTIST

 Look up the following passages where Jesus refers to John the Baptist as Elijah.

PASSAGE	NOTES
Matthew 11:13-14	
Matthew 17:11-13	
Mark 9:11-13	

These verses indicate that while the Holy Spirit is the one who fills John the Baptist, the specific quality of his influence will be to help John imitate Elijah in his wearing a camel-hair garment and leather belt (Elijah wore the same), and in his bold prophetic criticisms of kings (John against Herod, and Elijah against Ahab). All of this shows that the Holy Spirit will keep John in continuity with the Old Testament prophets as well as offer a specific kind of gift. This will be a characteristic of the Holy Spirit elsewhere in the New Testament.

CONSIDER

The Annunciation

The angel Gabriel makes known the role of the Holy Spirit in the incarnation of the Son of God in response to Mary's question, "How shall this be, since I have no husband?" (Lk 1:34). Unlike Zechariah, who wanted proof that he would have a son — "How shall I know this?" (Lk 1:18) — the Virgin Mary simply wants information on her next step of action.

 Stop here and read **Luke 1:30-38** in your own Bible.

The angel reveals that "The Holy Spirit will come upon you, and the power of the Most High will overshadow you" (Lk 1:35) so that this child will be called holy and will, in fact, be the Son of God. This indicates to Mary that the power of the Holy Spirit to create will take the place of that which a man would normally contribute to the conception of a child. This promise links the Holy Spirit to his creative role in Genesis, where he hovers over the waters. At the Incarnation, the action of the Holy Spirit renews the whole earth through the Word of God taking flesh in order to redeem all flesh from sin and, eventually, to make the whole earth new.

Parallel to the phrase "The Holy Spirit will come upon you" is the phrase "and the power of the Most High will overshadow you." This phrase confirms that the Holy Spirit is the "power of the Most High," which is one of the names of God going back to Abram and Melchizedek. The image of overshadowing presence is also found in the Old Testament as a reference to God overshadowing the Ark of the Covenant and the meeting tent when they were first constructed, and in order to indicate the need for Israel to remain in a particular place rather than move on. This presence of God in the overshadowing cloud was so powerful that the priests could not stand to be inside the Temple when the presence of God arrived in the cloud.

Interestingly, what the priests were too weak to bear, the Virgin Mary is able to bear within her womb. Her holiness outweighs their office.

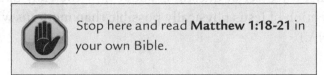

Stop here and read **Matthew 1:18-21** in your own Bible.

Joseph and the Spirit

While Luke presents the role of the Holy Spirit in the context of the angel Gabriel's dialogue with the Virgin Mary announcing the birth of the Son of God and the overshadowing power of the Holy Spirit that made the conception possible without the involvement of a man, Matthew presents the same role of the Holy Spirit in retrospect.

Matthew first explains this situation to the reader in an editorial notification, saying that "before they came together she was found to be with child of the Holy Spirit" (Mt 1:18). This form of writing lets the reader in on the story of Jesus' conception in preparation for the story of Joseph hearing about it. He also lets the reader know that Joseph is able to respond only to the external facts he can observe: his betrothed, Mary, is clearly with child, but he is absolutely certain that he is not the father. He can only surmise that she has been unfaithful to him, and he plans to act accordingly, though with a righteous mercy that covers both the legal requirement to divorce her and yet protect her from public shame. This resolution solves the problem of Joseph's love for the Law and his love for Mary, in spite of her apparent infidelity.

The second explanation of the Holy Spirit's role occurs in the angel's dialogue with Joseph, explaining that the child "which is conceived in her is of the Holy Spirit" (Mt 1:20). No description of the conception is offered, but simply a statement of the Holy Spirit's power to cause a conception within the womb of a faithful virgin.

In these first episodes in the life of Jesus, the Holy Spirit is presented as someone with creative power that makes procreation possible apart from a man's participation. Such creative power would make sense to Joseph and Mary in the context of believing the role of the Spirit of God in creating the world. (They might have had a less sophisticated set of questions about how the Holy Spirit made the conception of Jesus physically possible than moderns who know about DNA.)

STUDY

The Baptism of the Lord

The three Synoptic Gospels (Matthew, Mark, and Luke) emphasize the Trinitarian aspect of Jesus' baptism. The heavens "opened," followed by the Holy Spirit descending in the form of a dove and the Father speaking a description of Jesus as "my beloved Son, with whom I am well pleased" (Mt 3:17). This is the first public manifestation of the Blessed Trinity, at least in the sense that the three Persons are manifest at the same moment: the Son emerges from the waters of the Jordan; the Holy Spirit descends upon him; and the Father speaks his love of the Son. The Father and the Holy Spirit focus their complete attention on the Son, thereby indicating the harmony and unity between them.

INVESTIGATE

THE BAPTISM OF JESUS

 Look up the following passages and note the similarities and differences among them regarding Jesus' baptism.

PASSAGE	NOTES
Matthew 3:13-17	

Mark 1:9-11	
Luke 3:21-22	
John 1:32-34	

While John's Gospel does not include a narrative describing the baptism of Jesus, it does have a retrospective retelling both of the descent of the Holy Spirit upon Jesus and of a prophetic word that John the Baptist would recognize the Messiah by seeing the Holy Spirit descend upon him. In distinction from the Synoptic descriptions, a few details can be noted. First, unlike the Synoptics, John does not mention the Father's words. Second, none of the Synoptics mention that John had been told by the one "who sent me to baptize with water" (Jn 1:33) that he should expect to see the Spirit descend on the chosen one. The identity of the one who sent him is not made explicit, but is presumed to be God.

The most noteworthy point is that John the Baptist here emphasizes twice, both in his testimony and in his report of the prophecy, that the Holy Spirit descended and *remained* on Jesus. The evangelist does not indicate how John the Baptist knew that the Holy Spirit remained on Jesus, but he notes this as the criterion that Jesus is the one who "baptizes with the Holy Spirit" and is "the Son of God" (Jn 1:33, 34). The recognition that Jesus "baptizes with the Holy Spirit" is another element common in all four Gospels to John the Baptist's preaching about Jesus. The Baptist's identification of Jesus as the "Son of God" is unique to John.

STUDY

Temptations in the Wilderness

Only the three Synoptic Gospels mention Jesus' temptation in the wilderness, and all three agree that Jesus was "led" or was driven by the Spirit into the desert to be tempted by the devil or Satan. No direct link is made between Jesus' fast and the Holy Spirit, but all three agree that the Holy Spirit led him to be tempted by the evil spirit.

Three points must be made about this. First, no text says that the Holy Spirit tempted Jesus. It is clear that the devil/Satan tempted Jesus, not the Holy Spirit. In fact, Scripture explicitly denies that God ever tempts anyone: "Let no one say when he is tempted, 'I am tempted by God'; for God cannot be tempted with evil and he himself tempts no one; but each person is tempted when he is lured and enticed by his own desire" (Jas 1:13-14).

The second point can be made on the basis of a common question: If God tempts no one, then why did the Holy Spirit lead Jesus out to be tempted? The answer may be understood on the basis of an analogy. Military generals never want their soldiers to get killed. They oversee their training and equipping, so they want the soldiers to be well cared for in camp. However, when danger arises, a general leads his army into battle, not to be killed but to defeat the enemy. Similarly, the Holy Spirit led Jesus into the desert to engage the enemy of our souls in combat; not to harm Jesus but to let Jesus defeat the devil, who is the enemy of our souls.

The third point helps us make better sense of the conclusion of the Lord's Prayer, "Lead us not into temptation." Jesus knew precisely what it was like to be led into temptation, so he taught all his disciples to pray that they not undergo that test. This, too, is parallel to combat-hardened soldiers: they know better than any civilians who have never been in war how dangerous and terrible battle can be. Similarly, Jesus knows how horrid the temptations from the devil are, so he teaches us to pray that the Father lead us not into those temptations. If the Lord should lead us into situations of temptation, then we must struggle mightily against it, as Jesus did. But we can surely pray not to be so tempted.

INVESTIGATE

THE TEMPTATIONS OF JESUS

 Look up the following passages and make notes on the details given about the temptations, such as when Jesus was hungry.

PASSAGE	NOTES
Matthew 4:1-2	
Mark 1:12-13	
Luke 4:1-2	

CONSIDER

Jesus' Preaching Mission

While John's Gospel tells of Jesus attending a wedding at Cana immediately after his return from his baptism and the unmentioned temptations, Luke writes that right after the immediately preceding temptations, Jesus went to Nazareth. Since Nazareth is only five-and-a-half miles south of Cana, these two Gospels present a consistent picture of a journey from baptism and temptation in Judea to the first preaching and miracle in his home area in central Galilee.

The first point to notice is that the same Holy Spirit who led Jesus into the wilderness to be tempted now continues to lead him in power. The defeat of Satan's temptations empowers Jesus as he preaches throughout the synagogues of the region.

The second point is that when he attends the Sabbath service in the synagogue in Nazareth, he takes the initiative to stand up and read, and to passively receive the Isaiah scroll, from which he actively chooses to read Isaiah 61:1-2.

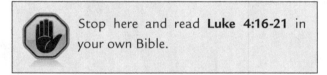

Stop here and read **Luke 4:16-21** in your own Bible.

Jesus makes the public announcement that his ministry is taking place by the power of the Holy Spirit. He does this in the synagogue where he grew up and where he probably learned how to read and write. Importantly, he announces that the Spirit of the Lord is upon him by citing Isaiah so that the newness of his present ministry can be understood in terms of an Old Testament prophecy, which the people are accustomed to hearing, since Isaiah is part of the yearly cycle of readings in the synagogue. Though his ministry perplexes and amazes them, he gives them a handle on the power of the Holy Spirit working through him.

As the rest of this chapter indicates, the people did not understand him and wanted to kill him. Yet, the words of Isaiah laid out the program of Jesus' ministry, not only in demonstrating the power of the Holy Spirit but also showing that Jesus will minister as Isaiah said he would — reaching out to the poor, giving sight to the blind, and announcing the great jubilee of redemption — and that he will do even more, such as raising the dead, feeding the multitudes, and rising from the dead himself.

STUDY

Victories Over Demons

Even during his public ministry, Jesus sent the Twelve Apostles on a preaching mission and then seventy other disciples in preparation for his arrival in the towns of Galilee. When the seventy returned, they were filled with joy that the demons were subject to his name when they spoke it.

 Stop here and read **Luke 9-10** in your own Bible.

Notice Jesus' response. He sees their victories over demons in terms of the great battle against Satan, who is losing his power and is falling. Then he gives them the true reason to rejoice: their "names are written in heaven" (Lk 10:20). Their victories over demons are not as important as the eternal life he can bestow on them for their faithfulness to him and his mission.

At that point, Jesus himself is filled with joy in the Holy Spirit, which directs him to thank his Father:

> In that same hour he rejoiced in the Holy Spirit and said, "I thank you, Father, Lord of heaven and earth, that you have hidden these things from the wise and understanding and revealed them to infants; yes, Father, for such was your gracious will. All things have been delivered to me by my Father; and no one knows who the Son is except the Father, or who the Father is except the Son and any one to whom the Son chooses to reveal him." (Lk 10:21-22, RSV-SCE)

This passage reveals a certain element of the inner relationship of the Blessed Trinity. Just as the Father sent the Holy Spirit upon Jesus at the Jordan River and proclaimed his love for the Son, so here the Holy Spirit directs Jesus toward his love of the Father, thanking him for the precise mission he has received from the Father, which is now revealed to the simple "infants" who are his disciples. These are clues of the inner love of the Holy Trinity that helped St. Augustine to identify the Holy Spirit as the Person who is the infinite love between the Father and the Son.

CONSIDER

Immediately after Matthew's comment that Jesus fulfills Isaiah 42:1-4, he relates the Lord's exorcism of a "blind and dumb demoniac" (Mt 12:22) and the Pharisees' objection that Jesus exorcizes demons by Beelzebul. "Knowing their thoughts," as only God can, Jesus speaks out.

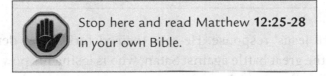

Stop here and read Matthew **12:25-28** in your own Bible.

The first part of Jesus' answer demonstrates the impossibility of Satan casting out Satan, or of the Lord casting out demons by Beelzebul. Therefore, the only logical conclusion is that Jesus casts out the evil spirits by the power of the Holy Spirit. However, this truth about the nature of his ministry by the power of the Holy Spirit has serious consequences for his listeners.

The Pharisees' attribution of the power of the Holy Spirit and its significance for the coming of the kingdom of God to Beelzebul is a blasphemy against the Holy Spirit. This attribution of evil to the power of God's own Spirit indicates a basic inability to recognize what God is doing. Such a blasphemy against the Holy Spirit is so serious a flaw within the soul that it cannot be forgiven.

STUDY

The Paraclete

Jesus states a few necessary steps that make it possible for the disciples to receive the Holy Spirit. Each disciple must love Jesus. Yet this love contains a major implication: they will keep his commandments as a fruit of loving Jesus. No one who loves another would want to offend that person. Therefore, to avoid offending the love Jesus has shown us disciples, we will do everything possible to keep his commandments.

The next step will be when he responds with yet more love toward those who keep the commandments: he will ask the heavenly Father to give them the Counselor, who is the Spirit of Truth. The answer to Jesus' prayer to the Father will be another Paraclete, or Counselor.

Stop and read **John 14:6, 16-17** in your own Bible.

Jesus uses the word "another" before Counselor, or Paraclete, which means that the disciples already have a Paraclete, namely,

PARAKLETOS

The Greek word *parakletos* etymologically means "someone called to one's side." A "paraclete" was a Greek term for an adviser, advocate, or counselor for the defense in a law court — that is, a defense lawyer. English and other languages still use the terms "counselor" or "advocate" as synonyms for lawyers. Just to make sure that lawyers do not get carried away with the loftiness of their profession on account of their "titles" being used as terms for the Holy Spirit, it is good to remind them at this point that both the Hebrew word *satan* and the Greek word *diabolos* (devil) mean prosecuting attorney in their respective languages.

Jesus himself. However, here he promises to ask the Father to give this other Paraclete to "be with you for ever" and to "be in you" (Jn 14:16-17). The character of this Paraclete is to be "the Spirit of truth," having two characteristics. First, he is an invisible Spirit, which enables him to enter within the heart and mind of the disciple who loves and obeys Jesus. Second, he is characterized by truth. However, since Jesus already identified himself as "the way, and the truth, and the life" (Jn 14:6), it is obvious that the Spirit of truth is closely connected to Jesus the truth.

This identification of the Spirit with truth does offer some explanation of why "the world cannot receive [him], because it neither sees him nor knows him" (Jn 14:17): the world has been incapable of accepting the truth who is Jesus, so it will certainly be incapable of accepting the Spirit of truth.

 Stop here and read **John 14:25-26** and **15:26-27** in your own Bible.

Jesus again states that the Father will send the Paraclete/Counselor, the Holy Spirit, but adds that he will send the Spirit in Jesus' "name" — that is, by the authority of Jesus. This passage places all three Persons of the Trinity in mutual cooperation. Yet, Jesus specifies that the Holy Spirit will have two particular tasks: first, he will teach the disciples, who love and obey Jesus in all things; and second, he will remind the disciples of everything Jesus had already said. These words imply that there is no conflict or divergence between "all things" the Holy Spirit will teach and everything that Jesus has already taught. These are in complete harmony.

Jesus' Revelations of the Spirit

 Stop here and read **John 16:5-15** in your own Bible.

Jesus begins this particular discussion about the Holy Spirit with an announcement of his return "to him who sent me" (Jn 16:5) — that is, the Father. While sensitive to the disciples' reaction to his departure, Jesus uses this as an opportunity to explain that his absence is an advantage to them because it means he can and will send the Paraclete/Counselor to them. This statement is an insight into the theology of the ascension of Jesus: it is not simply about ascending away from earth, where contact with Jesus would be limited only to those who could travel to the place where he is physically located. Rather, the Ascension to the "right hand of the Father" makes possible the descent of the Holy Spirit.

Another important point to notice is that Jesus explicitly states, "I will send" the Holy Spirit Counselor (Jn 16:7). In John 14:16 and 26, it says that the Father will send the Holy Spirit; in John 15:26 and 16:7, Jesus says he will send the Holy Spirit. The important thing to note is that Jesus does what the Father does: both send the Holy Spirit and neither sends him in contradiction to the other or without the other. These verses indicate that the great act of loving self-giving by God involves all three Persons of the Trinity in complete, total, and infinite union with one another.

The second section of this reading treats three tasks the Holy Spirit will accomplish when he comes to the disciples. Earlier, Jesus had spoken about the Spirit of truth "whom the world cannot receive, because it neither sees him nor knows him" (Jn 14:17). The inability

CONVINCING THE WORLD

The Greek word *elenchein* is here translated with the Latin form "convince"; some translators prefer "convict," which is from the same Latin root but uses a past perfect form to indicate that a person was already convinced. A more Anglo-Saxon translation is "prove wrong," since the goal of the verb here is not to sway an opinion but to demonstrate the falsehood of the world in the face of the Holy Spirit's truth. He will convict them of their wrongness — a function of the Holy Spirit's legal role as Paraclete for the disciples of Jesus Christ, but the one who convicts sinners and promoters of falsehood.

of the world to receive the Spirit of truth is not solely because of ignorance but also because of an animosity, similar to the hatred that the world has for Jesus, who is himself the truth.

The tension between the Spirit of truth and the world will increase the more he exercises his threefold ministry to the world: convincing the world "concerning sin and righteousness and judgment" (Jn 16:8).

How is the world wrong, then, about "sin and righteousness and judgment"?

First, the Holy Spirit will prove the world wrong about sin, "because they do not believe in me [Jesus]" (Jn 16:9). Throughout the Gospel of John, Jesus calls people to believe in him.

INVESTIGATE

BELIEVING IN JESUS

 Look up the following passages and make notes on what John says about believing in Jesus.

PASSAGE	NOTES
John 1:12	
John 3:16	

John 5:24	
John 6:29	
John 6:47	

However, the world rejected faith in Jesus and came to hate him, showing that neutrality toward Jesus is impossible. Rejection of faith in Jesus necessarily becomes a rejection of love for him and therefore is hatred, and as such is their most basic sin. The Holy Spirit will convict them that ultimately they were wrong for their rejection of Jesus.

Second, the Holy Spirit will convict the world "concerning righteousness, because I go to the Father, and you will see me no more" (Jn 16:10). The key to understanding this verse is in the meaning of "righteousness." In the Old Testament, it can mean moral correctness or being correct in regard to a set standard, as when weights and measures are righteous, and it can mean "innocence" in a legal trial. Israelites did not decree a person "guilty" or "not guilty," as in English common law; rather, they declared the guilty person to be "wicked" and the innocent person to be "righteous." The Holy Spirit will prove that Jesus is "righteous" or innocent of the charges of blasphemy that had been laid against him. Though little of Jesus' trials before the high priests Annas and Caiaphas are included in John's Gospel, the trial before Pilate is detailed, portraying it as a trial of Jesus by the "world." There the Jewish leaders accuse Jesus of blasphemy because he "made himself the Son of God" (Jn 19:7). Jesus' condemnation to crucifixion, an accursed way of dying, was supposed to prove that he was not the Son of God. However, Jesus rose from the dead and ascended to the Father, which vindicated him and proved him innocent, or righteous, of the false accusations of blasphemy. The Holy Spirit will therefore convict the world and prove them wrong about Jesus' righteous innocence.

Third, the Holy Spirit will convict the world "concerning judgment, because the ruler of this world is judged" (Jn 16:11). This third conviction of the world about judgment is a continuation of the Holy Spirit's role as Paraclete/Counselor, in which the one who comes to the defense of the disciples as their defense lawyer, or counselor, will work to convict the wrong judgment of the world. The key to understanding his conviction of the world's judgment can be found in Jesus' words on Palm Sunday:

> "Now is the judgment of this world, now shall the ruler of this world be cast out; and I, when I am lifted up from the earth, will draw all men to myself." He said this to show by what death he was to die. (Jn 12:31-33)

The determining issue is Jesus' being "lifted up" to die on the cross, which is the judgment of the world and the loss of power for the "ruler of this world," who is Satan. When Jesus is on trial in John's Gospel, the crowd demands that Pilate crucify Jesus — that is, lift him up on the tree. When Pilate asks, "Shall I crucify your king?" the high priests respond, "We have no king but Caesar" (Jn 19:15). While the crowd condemns Jesus to death and Pilate acquiesces, they proclaim loyalty to Caesar, whom they regard as the king of the world. However, the Holy Spirit will convict the world that, in fact, Satan is the "ruler of this world," as is clear in Jesus' temptations in the wilderness. The Holy Spirit will prove wrong all those who condemned Jesus to death, especially when he rises again and defeats the "ruler of this world." The Paraclete will prove that Jesus' words about the devil are the truth and that the world is wrong.

Later, John will write in his first epistle about the effect of the Holy Spirit's conviction of the world's judgment and the loss of power for Satan, the "ruler of this world."

INVESTIGATE

"THE RULER OF THIS WORLD"

 Look up the following passages and make notes on what is said about Satan.

PASSAGE	NOTES
1 John 2:13-14	
I John 4:4	
1 John 5:4-5	

Jesus Christ's disciples will receive a power to overcome the power of evil and the world. They must never forget the opposition and enmity that the world offers, and neither can they allow themselves to forget that Jesus has conquered evil. That will be the conviction that the Holy Spirit brings to their minds.

INVESTIGATE

THE DEFEAT OF EVIL

Look up the following passages and note anything that you find particularly revealing about the Spirit of God, the "ruler of the world," and the Second Coming.

PASSAGE	NOTES
Matthew 12:28	
2 Corinthians 4:4-5	
Ephesians 2:1-2	

Colossians 2:13-15	
Hebrews 2:14-15	
Revelation 12:9-11	

STUDY

Guidance into Truth

Jesus opens this section by notifying the disciples, who have been listening to him and learning from him for three years, that he still had much to teach them.

 Stop here and read **John 16:12-15** in your own Bible.

The double part of this instruction is that they neither know everything yet nor are they even capable of accepting some of the truth they still need to learn. This prepares them for the attitude all disciples must have — namely, humility about their present state of knowledge about God. God's infinity makes the ocean look like a drop in the bucket. Yet the ocean remains huge to us humans, and our minds are like mere drinking glasses trying to take in God's infinity. True humility is not putting ourselves down or self-deprecation. Rather, it is the turn toward God, whose infinite immensity gives us true perspective on our smallness. Only as we realize how little we know can we go forward with the proper humility to ever learn more.

Next, Jesus informs the disciples that the Spirit of truth, about whom he had already spoken, would guide them into all truth. Notice that the authority of the Spirit of truth to guide them into all truth comes from the fact that he has received everything that belongs to Jesus and that Jesus has received everything he has from the Father. These statements highlight the dominant characteristic of the relationships within the Trinity as complete self-giving: each Person completely gives of himself. Since this applies to God, it means that the self-giving is inherently infinite: each Person gives infinitely of himself to the other Persons. The necessary other side of this coin is that each Person also infinitely receives the infinity given to him. No Person holds back anything, and no Person rejects anything from the other. This is the quality of the unity within the Blessed Trinity.

INVESTIGATE

UNITY WITH THE FATHER

 The unity of Jesus with the Father is stated in many places. Look up the following passages and make notes of the key actions of the Father and the Son.

PASSAGE	NOTES
Matthew 11:27	

Matthew 28:18	
Luke 10:22	
John 3:35	
John 10:29-30	
John 13:3	
John 17:1-2	

John 17:9-10	
Colossians 1:19	
Colossians 2:9	

In John 16:12-15, Jesus includes the Holy Spirit in the self-giving and accepting of God, thereby asserting that God is not a duality of Father and Son but a Trinity of three Persons absolutely one in their divinity, their infinite self-giving, and the acceptance of the others.

STUDY

The Holy Spirit Is God

The Christian community in Jerusalem had received a second common outpouring of the Holy Spirit, which not only strength-ened them in proclaiming the Gospel but also encouraged many to place all their property in common ownership and usage. This was freely done, but the people were inspired by the Holy Spirit to do so (Acts 4:23-37). However, one couple, Ananias and Sapphira, sold their property and claimed to give it to the whole community, even though they were secretly withholding part. They were free to give it or not, but they were deceptive in their action.

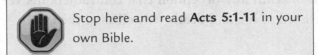
Stop here and read **Acts 5:1-11** in your own Bible.

Ananias died for telling a "lie to the Holy Spirit" (Acts 5:3), which Peter equates with lying to God. This extremely important passage indicates that Peter and the early Church understood Jesus' teaching about the Holy Spirit to mean that the Holy Spirit is truly God and truly a Person. Some sects, such as the fourth-century Arians and modern Jehovah's Witnesses, teach that the Holy Spirit is neither God nor a Person but simply a force that God uses to accomplish his will. However, if the Holy Spirit were an impersonal force, how could someone assert that he has been lied to? No one can tell a lie to the wind, sea, or earth; they do not have rational minds that can detect the truth from falsehood. Neither can the forces of nature decide to punish a person for a lie, as the Holy Spirit does in this passage. A poorly trained or foolish sailor or aviator might die for contradicting laws of nature, but not because nature chooses to single out one fool from another; all fools who sail or fly in ignorance endanger their lives. Here the Holy Spirit knows the truth from Ananias' and Sapphira's falsehood and chooses to punish them, exercising both rational intellect and free will, thereby indicating that he is truly a Person. This, of course, follows logically from Jesus' teaching that the Holy Spirit is the Spirit of truth.

Another point can be made about the Holy Spirit from Sapphira's decision to sustain her husband's lie. Peter says to her: "How is it that you have agreed together to tempt the Spirit of the Lord? Hark, the feet of those that have buried your husband are at the door, and they will carry you out" (Acts 5: 9). She died at that moment, causing "great fear" in the Church and in all who heard of it (Acts 5:11). The Lord God is the one who takes away someone's breath, causing the person to die, or sends his Spirit, causing them to die. Here, the Holy Spirit also shows his divine nature by demonstrating that human life is his to give and to take away. The early Christian community learned powerfully through this episode that no one ought to tell the

Holy Spirit of truth any deception that contradicts his very nature. He will be Lord of life and death, as well as of the truth.

CONSIDER

Grieving the Spirit

Paul also warned the Christian community that it is possible for the believers to "grieve" the Holy Spirit by committing immorality.

 Stop here and read **Ephesians 4:30-32** in your own Bible.

Paul admonishes the whole community (the verbs are all second-person plural) against grieving the Holy Spirit, in whom they were "sealed" for the day of redemption. The cause of the Holy Spirit's grief is bitterness, wrath, anger, clamor, slander, and malice — sins caused by evil intentions and words that aim to destroy another person's reputation and character. Here Paul understands the Holy Spirit as a Person who can experience grief and sadness over the sins committed by Christians. Another aspect of the Holy Spirit's Personhood is that he knows the difference between those vices of the interior attitude and the virtues of being kind, tenderhearted, and forgiving, just as God is. Only a person with intellect can discern the difference between the virtues and vices, and only a good person can become grieved over vice and joyful over virtue. In addition, these virtues and vices belong to interior decisions and attitudes of the will — interior choices deep within the conscience. The ability to read hearts is a quality of God (1 Sam 16:7; Jer 11:20; 17:10; 20:12), and this passage assumes that the Holy Spirit is God, capable of knowing the heart, exactly as Jesus (Jn 2:25).

Another way the Spirit is grieved is through sexual immorality. Paul calls the Thessalonians to the sanctification of their bodies by avoiding sins of lust, which were commonplace in Greco-Roman culture, and instead to live out authentic love.

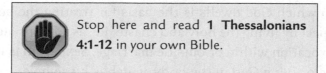
Stop here and read **1 Thessalonians 4:1-12** in your own Bible.

Paul makes absolutely clear that the summons to a chaste purity and holiness is not his or anyone else's mere human commandment but is God's. The prohibition of adultery includes all forms of chaste holiness that are appropriate for each state of life, whether married or unmarried. Any disregard of chaste living equates with disregard of God "who gives his Holy Spirit" (1 Thess 4:8) so that disciples can live out the holiness required in the area of sexual morality and authentic self-giving love.

Paul also wrote to the Corinthians in line with this theme of the Holy Spirit and sexual morality being linked to his divinity.

Stop here and read **1 Corinthians 3:16-20** in your own Bible.

The first statement of Paul's teaching is given in the context of his explanation that the Corinthians must not divide themselves into sects loyal to different teachers — Apollos, Cephas, Paul, or Christ. He then drives home his point that instead of dividing up into sects, they need to understand themselves as God's temple. In the Greek "you" is plural; the whole community is "God's temple and that God's Spirit dwells in you" (1 Cor 3:16). Yet, so also is each individual Christian a temple of the Holy Spirit, a point that has important ramifications for the moral life — namely, shunning immorality.

The "immorality" to be shunned here is *porneia* in Greek, the term for sexual immorality. He motivates Christians to avoid *porneia* (from which comes the English word pornography, or porno) by stating that the body of each Christian is a "temple of the Holy Spirit within you" (1 Cor 3:19). This tremendous dignity of being the temple in which God dwells is the basis for treating the body with great respect by living the holy and chaste life, as appropriate to each person's vocation within or outside marriage. Sexual sin is not irrelevant to glorifying God in the body, which is his temple.

These passages are all building blocks of Christian truth about the Holy Spirit, the Church as a whole, and the moral life of the individual Christian. First, in regard to the Holy Spirit: if the whole Church and each individual Christian is a "temple of the Holy Spirit," then we must conclude that he is truly God, to be adored within that temple. Israel was forbidden to make temples except the one temple of the Lord God in Jerusalem. Only God is to be adored in that temple. Paul's teaching that the temple of the Church and the individual Christian is a "temple of the Holy Spirit" means that the Holy Spirit is God. He is the object of our adoration in his temple, and nothing less is acceptable.

Second, the Holy Spirit is, in fact, associated with God in these passages about sexual morality and chastity. These texts identify the Holy Spirit as God, who must be obeyed and adored.

Third, the Holy Spirit, whom Jesus promised to send us in order to lead us into all truth (Jn 16:13), includes within his truth the summons to a holy and chaste purity regarding sexuality and the human body in general. Other truths of the rest of human morality and the truths about the doctrine of the faith are included, of course. However, the modern world, just like the Greco-Roman world, needs a reminder of the ways the Holy Spirit, the Giver of life, summons each and every human being to a holiness lived out in the body, the Spirit's temple, in order to give glory to God by our moral life.

DISCUSS

1. How can we be sure that the Holy Spirit is God, the third Person of the Trinity, from the passages cited in this session?
2. What new insights have you gained about the Temptation of the Lord from this study?
3. What does it mean to you to "grieve" the Holy Spirit?

PRACTICE

If you aren't accustomed to praying to the Holy Spirit directly, take some time this week to speak to the Spirit — asking for guidance, thanking for wisdom, and seeking understanding. Remember that through your baptism and confirmation, you have the Spirit dwelling within you, waiting and ready to be a part of your daily life.

Session 6

EMPOWERMENT IN THE NEW TESTAMENT

> "The grace of the Lord Jesus Christ and the love of God and the fellowship of the Holy Spirit be with you all."
> — 2 CORINTHIANS 13:14

As we saw in the Old Testament, the Holy Spirit is given to empower the prophets to speak the word of God. The same is true in the New Testament as well, and it begins from the time the Son of God is incarnate in the womb of his mother, the Virgin Mary of Nazareth. At this point, we will examine the three prophecies about Mary and Jesus in Luke's infancy narratives.

STUDY

The first occurs very soon after the Incarnation, when the Virgin Mary quickly goes to visit her kinswoman Elizabeth, who is herself six months with child.

Stop here and read **Luke 1:39-45** in your own Bible.

Both Elizabeth and her son in the womb are filled with the Holy Spirit at the approach of the Virgin Mary carrying the incarnate Son of God. Little John praises according to his ability and leaps inside his mother. Elizabeth is also "filled with the Holy Spirit" (Lk 1:41) as soon as she hears Mary's greeting and is inspired to proclaim three beatitudes. The first is directed to Mary, blessing her as the most blessed woman of all: "Blessed are you among women" (Lk 1:42). This is a Semitic expression of the superlative, stating that Mary is more blessed than any woman in history because she now bears the Messiah in her womb. The second beatitude, "blessed is the fruit of your womb" (Lk 1:42), is directed toward her son, Jesus. The third beatitude, "blessed is she who believed that there would be a fulfillment of what was spoken to her from the Lord" (Lk 1:45), is directed again to Mary for her faith in the naturally impossible act by which God causes the conception of a child in a virgin's womb.

Like most of the prophets, Elizabeth might not have had a complete understanding of the words she herself had spoken. The Holy Spirit was able to speak a mystery through her that exceeded her capacity at that moment. However, the meaning of the power of these words is such that the Church continues meditating on the words, especially the first two beatitudes used in the Hail Mary.

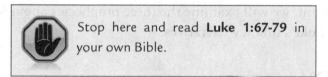

Stop here and read **Luke 1:67-79** in your own Bible.

The second prophetic word comes through Zechariah, who, after obeying the angel Gabriel's command to name his son "John," then is able to open his mouth and speak (Lk 1:63-64). He is at that moment filled with the Holy Spirit and prophesies with a hymn of praise for the Messiah within Mary's womb and for his son.

Only in verses 76-79 does Zechariah address his son, John. While Jesus is a horn of salvation from the house of David, as prophesied in the past, Zechariah's son, John, is a "prophet of the Most High." His task will be to precede Jesus and prepare his way by giving people knowledge of salvation through forgiveness of sins. Yet, even this section emphasizes that Christ is the rising dawn who will give light to those sitting in darkness and the shadow of death. Clearly, here the emphasis of the prophecy is on Jesus, who is just three months in his mother's womb.

 Stop here and read **Luke 2:25-32** in your own Bible.

The third prophecy occurs at the Presentation in the Temple, when Joseph and Mary come to Jerusalem to obey the law of purification of Mary and of an offering for her firstborn son, Jesus.

Note first that the elderly Simeon is already a righteous and devout man looking forward to the Messiah and sensitive to the presence of the Holy Spirit. Second, an earlier prophecy is mentioned, by which he received a personal revelation that he would see the Messiah before he died. Third, the Holy Spirit inspires him to enter the Temple precisely at the time when Joseph and Mary are fulfilling the commandments of God in regard to childbirth of a firstborn son. Fourth, as he picks up this child of these two Galilean strangers, he prophesies in a hymn of praise, acknowledging in faith that the Lord has fulfilled his promise by permitting him to see the infant Messiah. Rather than asking to see the complete defeat of the Romans or some other political action, he recognizes that he can die now, since the Lord has fulfilled his promise to "see" the Lord's Messiah, and not anything more than that.

Finally, after blessing Joseph and Mary, he addresses her with prophetic words about Jesus and her. First, the child "is set for the fall and rising of many in Israel, / and for a sign that is spoken against" (Lk 2:34). This prophecy forms one of the themes of the whole Gospel as we read of people falling by rejecting Jesus or rising to healing and peace through his ministry. The second part of his prophecy is addressed to the Virgin Mother: "A sword will pierce through your own soul also, / that thoughts out of many hearts may be revealed" (Lk 2:35).

CONSIDER

Baptism with the Spirit

Consistent with John the Baptist's humility about his role as the forerunner of Christ, his teaching regularly contrasts his baptismal ministry with the power of the Messiah to baptize "with the Holy Spirit."

INVESTIGATE

"WITH THE HOLY SPIRIT"

 Look up the following passages and make notes on baptism by the Spirit.

PASSAGE	NOTES
Mark 1:8	
Matthew 3:11-12	
Luke 3:16-17	

A couple points can be made here. First, Mark's passage, as is often the case, is much shorter, simply mentioning the contrast between John the Baptist's use of water and the power to baptize with the Holy Spirit. In none of the Synoptic Gospels does the Baptist explain what being baptized in the Holy Spirit means. He would have only the teachings of the Old Testament on the Holy Spirit to inform this teaching. However, John is certain that whatever God might mean about a baptism in the Holy Spirit, only the Messiah can give it, not John.

Second, in Matthew and Luke, John associates the "coming one's" power to baptize with the Holy Spirit with his power to judge people and their deeds with fire. John is only able to warn and exhort sinners to repent and cease their evil; the "coming one" will actually have a power to judge people.

STUDY

The Necessity of the Spirit

Jesus did not promise his disciples that their ministry would be filled only with success, love, and acceptance of them and the Gospel. Rather, from the beatitudes onward, he warned that they would be persecuted and would, like him, pick up their suffering for the sake of the Gospel in various ways. Among those sufferings would be arrest and trial. He instructed them not to be anxious about what they are to say, for the Spirit would speak through them. Jesus promised that they would receive the Holy Spirit, the "Spirit of your Father," and he would be doing the actual speaking.

 Stop here and read **Matthew 10:19**, **Mark 13:11**, and **Luke 12:8-12** in your own Bible.

STUDY

John's Gospel and the Spirit

John's Gospel primarily teaches through discourses, as seen in the Last Supper Discourse Jesus taught about the Holy Spirit's relation to the Father, the Son, and the disciples who would receive him. In three earlier discourses, mention of the promise of the Holy Spirit is made to people who had only the Old Testament understanding of God's Spirit. Their ideas about the Holy Spirit were not so clear and definite, so these discourses present general preparations for Jesus' fuller teaching on the Holy Spirit.

The first promise of the Holy Spirit occurs in Jesus' nighttime discourse with the Pharisee Nicodemus, where he explains that a person must be born again of water and the Spirit.

Stop here and read **John 3:1-21** in your own Bible.

Jesus introduces the Spirit here as the divine agent in baptism by water who makes it possible for a person to enter the kingdom of God. He contrasts the power of the Spirit with the human flesh, and he then offers a general teaching about the influence of the Spirit. The person born anew is like the wind, which blows without humans knowing its origin or final destination. However, not much else is said about the Holy Spirit himself — only his effects.

Stop here and read **John 3:25-35** in your own Bible.

The second discourse is with John the Baptist. Again, nothing is said about the Spirit but only that Jesus, the one "sent" by God, utters the "words of God" because God the Father gives his Son the Spirit without "measure" (Jn 3:34). This provides the background of faith for the day of the Resurrection, when Jesus will breathe the Holy Spirit upon the disciples: Jesus can give them the Holy Spirit because there is no limit to the Spirit given to Jesus so that he can bestow the Spirit upon believers.

Stop here and read **John 7:37-44** in your own Bible.

114

The Greek word translated as "heart" is *koilias*, which literally means "hollow," particularly the "hollow" of the body — that is, the thoracic cage containing the lungs and heart and the "lower hollow" containing the stomach, intestines, kidneys, liver, and spleen. The Septuagint uses it to translate terms ranging from belly, digestive system, womb, and heart, as well as the hidden human thoughts and desires. The last two meanings fit best here to explain Jesus' promise to those who believe in him. They will find a satisfaction to their own inner thirst from the person of Jesus Christ, such as he promised to the Samaritan woman at the well. John the Evangelist assumes that his readers might be as confused as the Samaritan woman or the crowd of people who heard them. Therefore, he explains that Jesus is referring to the Holy Spirit that Jesus will pour out after his glorification, when he rises from the dead.

CONSIDER

Jesus Bestows the Spirit

Though Jesus had appeared to other people on the day of resurrection, the most important meeting of the day occurred that evening in the upper room.

Stop here and read **John 20:19-23** in your own Bible.

Note that Jesus does not berate the disciples for running away in fear from Gethsemane nor for Peter's denial, but greets them with both peace and proof that the same person who was crucified and pierced in the side is the very Jesus standing alive in front of them. After a second extension of peace, Jesus sends the disciples just as the Father sent him, since Jesus does what the Father does. Therefore,

Jesus sends the disciples out on the same mission that he received to save the world.

Yet Jesus is fully aware that "the spirit is willing but the flesh is weak" (Mt 26:41, Mk 14:38), as he said to the same disciples in Gethsemane. Therefore, the disciples need another power for this mission and for the ministry of forgiving or retaining sins, so Jesus breathes the Holy Spirit upon them.

Jesus does not simply send them on a mission depending solely on their own human ability; the fact that he showed himself to the disciples while they were in a locked room out of fear of the people who had killed him indicates that they do not have much natural courage. The mission to go out to the world requires a strength that is beyond them, so Jesus breathes the Holy Spirit upon them in order to make them a "new creation." This is the same Holy Spirit whom he had designated as the Counselor who "will teach you all things, and bring to your remembrance all that I have said to you" (Jn 14:26), "the Spirit of truth, whom the world cannot receive" (Jn 14:17) and who "will guide you into all the truth" (Jn 16:13) and "bear witness" to Jesus (Jn 15:26), who is the truth (Jn 14:6).

These verses also indicate that the apostles will have true authority to forgive sins, but not by human cleverness or personal strength of character. Rather, they will have this power to forgive or retain the sins of those who confess to them by the Holy Spirit. God the Holy Spirit will give that gift and guarantee its effectiveness. For that reason, people who blaspheme the Holy Spirit by denying his ability to empower true forgiveness of sins are designated by Jesus as those who cannot be forgiven: they have sinned against the Holy Spirit.

CONSIDER

The Gift of the Spirit

Luke's second book, the Acts of the Apostles, relates how the promised Holy Spirit was bestowed upon the early Church. Though this gift began with the circle of the Twelve Apostles, the Holy Spirit was given to the larger community of Jewish disciples and then to Christians everywhere the Gospel of Jesus Christ was preached.

In the introduction of Acts, Luke says, "I have dealt with all that Jesus began to do and teach, until the day when he was taken up, after he had given commandment through the Holy Spirit to the apostles whom he had chosen" (Acts 1:1-2).

> Stop here and read **Luke 1:1-8** in your own Bible.

Luke reminds his readers that the Gospel was about Jesus' actions and teachings, while this second book begins with his teaching to the apostles after his resurrection. Just as Jesus had recognized the power of the Holy Spirit at the beginning of his ministry, so also here it states that Jesus' commands, or commission, to the apostles were given "through the Holy Spirit."

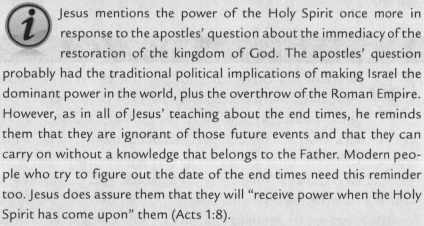

THE KINGDOM OF GOD

Jesus mentions the power of the Holy Spirit once more in response to the apostles' question about the immediacy of the restoration of the kingdom of God. The apostles' question probably had the traditional political implications of making Israel the dominant power in the world, plus the overthrow of the Roman Empire. However, as in all of Jesus' teaching about the end times, he reminds them that they are ignorant of those future events and that they can carry on without a knowledge that belongs to the Father. Modern people who try to figure out the date of the end times need this reminder too. Jesus does assure them that they will "receive power when the Holy Spirit has come upon" them (Acts 1:8).

The first evidence of that power will not be knowledge of the future but a power to witness to Jesus and all that he has said and done. Their future will concern explaining and proclaiming the past of Jesus' redemption. The rest of the power that the Holy Spirit will give remains an unknown mystery to them at this point, but it, too, will be made manifest as they go forth into the world as Jesus' witnesses in word and deed.

Next, "while staying" (literally "sharing salt with" — that is, "eating meals") with the apostles, Jesus commanded them to remain in Jerusalem so they could be "baptized with the Holy Spirit."

Note that this baptism in the Holy Spirit is here identified as "the promise of the Father," which Jesus had made earlier in his ministry.

STUDY

Pentecost

Luke describes the coming of the Holy Spirit at Pentecost as a mighty wind and tongues of fire.

In the upper room, the Holy Spirit was manifested in flames of pure fire without smoke or thick cloud, and the flames parted like tongues of fire upon each person in order to enter within the person and fill each one with the Holy Spirit. The Lord was in the fire and wind in order to empower the early Christians and not simply to speak to each individual. They "were all filled with the Holy Spirit" (Acts 2:4) and received power because of the Spirit's dwelling within each one.

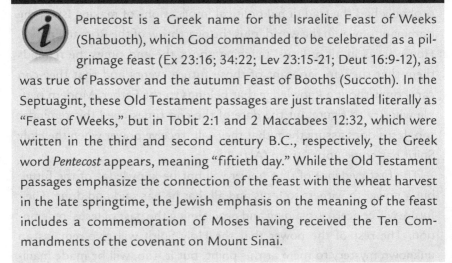

FEAST OF WEEKS

Pentecost is a Greek name for the Israelite Feast of Weeks (Shabuoth), which God commanded to be celebrated as a pilgrimage feast (Ex 23:16; 34:22; Lev 23:15-21; Deut 16:9-12), as was true of Passover and the autumn Feast of Booths (Succoth). In the Septuagint, these Old Testament passages are just translated literally as "Feast of Weeks," but in Tobit 2:1 and 2 Maccabees 12:32, which were written in the third and second century B.C., respectively, the Greek word *Pentecost* appears, meaning "fiftieth day." While the Old Testament passages emphasize the connection of the feast with the wheat harvest in the late springtime, the Jewish emphasis on the meaning of the feast includes a commemoration of Moses having received the Ten Commandments of the covenant on Mount Sinai.

The first experience of the Holy Spirit's power was their ability "to speak in other tongues, as the Spirit gave them utterance" (Acts 2:4), a gift that would serve them well with the crowd gathering outside the upper room because of the sound of the loud wind. However, this would be the mere beginning of the signs of power and prophecy, which the Acts of the Apostles continues to tell.

 Stop here and read **Acts 2:5-13** and **2:14-36** in your own Bible.

Luke describes the response of the crowds — ranging from amazement to cynicism, followed by Peter's bold sermon. The first part of this sermon explains this manifestation of the Holy Spirit in terms of the fulfillment of Old Testament prophecy. Peter then cites an eschatological prophecy explaining that God will pour his Spirit upon all flesh "in the last days" (Acts 2:17).

The rest of the prophecy makes two points. The first emphasis is on the effects of God's Spirit on people of both genders and of every stage and station in life. They will know things beyond the limits of their own minds through revelations in dreams and prophecies. The second emphasis is on the signs of "the day of the Lord" (Acts 2:20), the Old Testament term for the end of time. Not only does the resurrection of Jesus initiate a "new creation," but also the outpouring of the Holy Spirit initiates the process leading to the end of time.

After explaining the manifestation of the Holy Spirit as the fulfillment of prophecy, Peter goes on to connect the coming of the Holy Spirit with the ministry, death, and resurrection of Jesus of Nazareth.

 Stop here and read **Acts 2:37-39** in your own Bible.

Peter again mentions the Father's gift of the Holy Spirit to the apostles, who are witnesses of the Resurrection and exaltation at the right hand of the Father, from where Jesus poured out the Holy Spirit he had received. In conclusion, Peter exhorts the listeners to repent and be baptized in the name of Jesus for the forgiveness of sins. These are the preconditions for the international crowd to receive the same gift of the Holy Spirit as the apostles and disciples have received. Not only is the gift promised to them but also to their descendants and to every person, near or far, who accepts God's call.

STUDY

Peter and John on Trial

After a man born lame was healed in the name of Jesus, Peter and John were arrested and forced to stand trial before the Sanhedrin. The man who ran from the soldiers in Gethsemane and denied Jesus during his trial before the Sanhedrin is now filled with the Holy Spirit, as he himself is on trial before the same Sanhedrin.

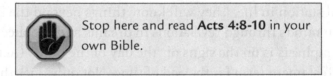 Stop here and read **Acts 4:8-10** in your own Bible.

The Holy Spirit gives Peter a boldness he completely failed to demonstrate on his own personal strength in Gethsemane and in Caiaphas' court. The Holy Spirit gives him the words to speak during his trial, exactly as Jesus promised.

After their first trial before the Sanhedrin, Peter and John return to the rest of the Christian community and relate the events. Their response to the news of the healing, the 3,000 conversions to Jesus Christ, and the outcome of the trial was to raise their voices in prayer together.

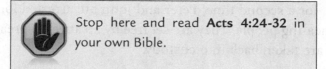

Stop here and read **Acts 4:24-32** in your own Bible.

Their prayer, first of all, recognizes that the same Holy Spirit they received on Pentecost and by which they healed and preached in the name of Jesus Christ had also inspired "our father David" (Acts 4:25) to compose Psalm 2. They understand the arrest, trial, and execution of Jesus through that prophetic lens, even to the point of seeing Pilate and Herod as taking their roles in the fulfillment of this psalm. This is the same lens through which they understand their own present trial — it is not failure but a challenge for which they seek increased boldness to continue speaking the Lord's word.

To this prayer, the Lord responds with another outpouring of the Holy Spirit, similar to Pentecost, with a shaking of the room and another filling of the Holy Spirit, who gave them the boldness they prayed for. In addition, the Holy Spirit gives them an increased unity among themselves, not exteriorly but making the believers "one heart and soul" (Acts 4:32). They even share their property in common with one another.

This episode indicates that the gift of the Holy Spirit being poured out is not simply a onetime event in the life of the Christian community nor in the experience of individuals. New circumstances sometimes evoke a greater outpouring and still more gifts of the Holy Spirit: in this case, greater boldness and a willingness to share their lives to the point of sharing private property for the sake of the community's needs.

(Throughout the history of the Church, in good times and especially in times of tepidity, the Holy Spirit has renewed the Church with the outpouring of new gifts and charisms, along with deeper community life through the establishment of new religious orders and communities. The charism usually comes through one individual, but it spreads to others who then form the new community. In this way, the Church remains ever new and renewed throughout its history.)

Next, for a second time, Peter and John are arrested for preaching and healing people. They are set free by an angel to preach again but then are taken back into custody.

 Stop here and read **Acts 5:12-32** in your own Bible.

At that point, Peter again addresses the Sanhedrin with a simple proclamation of the Gospel of Jesus. Interestingly, Peter announces that both he and John are witnesses to Jesus' death and resurrection for the repentance and forgiveness of sins in Israel, and the Holy Spirit, whom God has given to those who obey him, is witness too. The Holy Spirit gives his witness precisely through Peter, John, and the apostles, "those who obey" God (Acts 5:32), by their words of true proclamation, by their miracles and healings, and by their boldness before the Sanhedrin.

CONSIDER

The First Deacons and the Holy Spirit

The early Christian community was not without tensions and difficulties, as seen when the Greek-speaking Jews (the "Hellenists") "murmured against the Hebrews" (Aramaic- and Hebrew-speaking Jews) because "their widows were neglected in the daily distribution" of food (Acts 6:1). The solution was the establishment of the diaconate, a new office in the Church to help the Twelve by taking care of the distribution of food.

 Stop here and read **Acts 6:1-11** in your own Bible.

The apostles invited the Hellenists to choose the seven deacons. All seven were all to be "men of good repute, full of the Spirit and of wisdom" (Acts 6:3). All seven were expected to be full of the Holy Spirit, along with specific other gifts and fruit of the Holy Spirit — particularly wisdom and faith, plus a good reputation, which was indicative of other virtues observable by all. Stephen was especially singled out as "a man full of faith and of the Holy Spirit" (Acts 6:5).

Though the deacons were originally chosen to distribute food and supplies evenly to the widows and other needy members of the community, their gifts also opened them to other aspects of ministry. This is seen first with Stephen, who engaged members of the "synagogue of the Freedmen" (of which some ruins have been found in Jerusalem) in debates and apologetics about Jesus Christ (Acts 6:9).

The important notice here is that the "wisdom and the Spirit" (Acts 6:10), which were reasons to choose Stephen as a deacon, are able to thwart any of the reasons and arguments brought against the Christian faith by the members of the "synagogue of Freedmen." In the face of their inability to refute Stephen's "wisdom and the Spirit," they can sustain their antagonism toward him only by instigating false witnesses, just as had been done to Jesus at his trial before the Sanhedrin.

After his arrest, Stephen gave a long trial speech — the longest in the Acts of the Apostles — to defend what he had said.

 Stop here and read **Acts 7:1-56** in your own Bible.

In the face of his accusers' anger and rage, Stephen remains "full of the Holy Spirit" (Acts 7:55), which then opens him to a vision of heaven, God's glory, and Jesus standing at God's right hand — a fulfillment of Psalm 110:1: "The LORD said to my lord: / 'Sit at my right hand, / till I make your enemies your footstool.'" Such a vision of heaven is a grace that God the Holy Spirit bestows, in this case on someone who is in the same kind of danger of death as Jesus was during his trial. In fact, Stephen was led out of Jerusalem and stoned to death, with the complicity of a certain Saul. Stephen is helped to die with the same attitude and words of Jesus. This, too, is the wisdom and power of the Holy Spirit at work within Stephen until he breathes his last before entering the very heaven the Holy Spirit enabled him to see at the end of his trial.

STUDY

The Holy Spirit in Samaria

Philip, one of the six deacons who survived the persecution after the martyrdom of Stephen the deacon, went to Samaria to preach the Gospel, just as Jesus had commanded, and he baptized many people. However, Philip did not have the authority to bestow the Holy Spirit on the newly baptized, so Peter and John were summoned to Samaria.

 Stop here and read **Acts 8:14-17** in your own Bible.

Their purpose was to pray for the Samaritans that "they might receive the Holy Spirit" (Acts 8:15). The use of the subjunctive shows that the apostles are not in control of the Holy Spirit; theirs was not a magical power that could control God. Rather, it was an exercise of trusting faith that God would continue to extend the gift of the Holy Spirit even beyond the community of Jews to the otherwise rather hated community of Samaritans.

A second point to note here is that baptism "in the name of the Lord Jesus" (Acts 8:16) was not sufficient to receive the Holy Spirit in power. For that reason, the two apostles laid hands upon each person, and they received the Holy Spirit. Philip, as a deacon, did not have the authority to lay hands on the people for this; he could preach and baptize, but not pass on this gift. Because of this example of behavior in the early Church, deacons still have the ministry of preaching and baptizing, but the bishop and the priests he designates are the ordinary ministers of Confirmation, the sacrament in which a person receives the outpouring of the Holy Spirit.

Buying the Spirit?

While the people of Samaria experienced conversion, a new problem arose when a popular local magician named Simon (nicknamed "Magus" for being a magician) wanted to purchase the power to bestow the Holy Spirit. He had been quite impressed with his own powers, and the Samaritans called his "the power of God." Even though he believed and was baptized, he was more amazed at the miracles and power manifested through Philip (Acts 8:9-13).

Stop here and read **Acts 8:18-24** in your own Bible.

After Simon's offer of money to buy the power of bestowing the Holy Spirit, Simon Peter strongly rebukes Simon Magus for trying to buy God's gift. Such a thought indicated that Simon Magus did not have a right heart; he was still too impressed with himself and with wonders that diverted his attention away from God, the giver of the gift.

We do well to consider the words, "Even Simon himself believed, and after being baptized he continued with Philip" (Acts 8:13). Many Christians teach that a person is saved by faith alone, and that once a person is saved the salvation cannot be lost ("Once saved, always saved"). However, Simon Magus believed and was baptized, but he fell into a grave sin that required Peter to call him to "repent" because of being "in the gall of bitterness and in the bond of iniquity" (Acts 8:23) that still held him. If he did not repent, he could lose his salvation, as his prayer indicates in Acts 8:24 that "nothing of what you have said may come upon me."

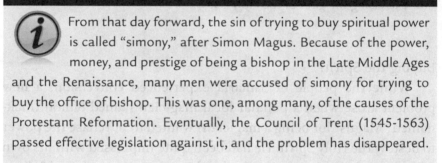

SIMONY

From that day forward, the sin of trying to buy spiritual power is called "simony," after Simon Magus. Because of the power, money, and prestige of being a bishop in the Late Middle Ages and the Renaissance, many men were accused of simony for trying to buy the office of bishop. This was one, among many, of the causes of the Protestant Reformation. Eventually, the Council of Trent (1545-1563) passed effective legislation against it, and the problem has disappeared.

STUDY

The Spirit and Paul

Stop here and read **Acts 9:1-19** in your own Bible.

After the young Pharisee Saul is overpowered by a vision of Jesus on the road to Damascus, he is now blind and is brought into Damascus, where he prays and fasts from food and water for three days. After three days, the Lord appears to a Christian named Ananias, who is instructed to go to Saul. Though reluctant because of Saul's intention to arrest him and other Christians, he obeys the Lord and goes to Saul.

Ananias initiates the conversation both by laying hands on Saul and addressing him as "Brother," thereby indicating his readiness to include Saul in the Christian community (Acts 9:17). The double purpose of the laying on of hands is to heal Saul and for him to be "filled with the Holy Spirit" (Acts 9:17). Though Saul has turned away from his plan to persecute and destroy the Church because of Jesus' appearance to him, he still does not have the positive faith to believe. That will require the movement of the Holy Spirit within him. Certainly this experience would affect his later teaching that "no one can say 'Jesus is Lord' except by the Holy Spirit" (1 Cor 12:3) and "When we cry, 'Abba! Father!' it is the Spirit himself bearing witness with our spirit that we are children of God" (Rom 8:15-16).

Ananias prayed for healing of Saul's blindness and baptized him — both a physical and spiritual removal of blindness. This began a total conversion by which Saul becomes Paul (a name change because the Greek form of his Hebrew name, *Saulos*, means "effeminate"), who is filled with the Holy Spirit and manifests his power in words, deeds, and eventually in writing a number of books that are the inspired word of God, Sacred Scripture.

First Gentile Convert

The story of the conversion of the first gentile from paganism to Christianity is central to the whole of the Acts of the Apostles. All of the previous converts came from Judaism. However, the centurion Cornelius was the first pagan convert.

 Stop here and read **Acts 10:1-48** in your own Bible.

God takes the initiative in Cornelius' conversion by sending him an angel, who instructs him to call for Peter. Meanwhile, Peter is prepared for this visit by a thrice-repeated vision commanding him to eat unclean — that is, unkosher — foods. Finally, Peter goes to Caesarea Maritima and preaches to Cornelius about Jesus, during which sermon the Holy Spirit comes upon Cornelius and his whole household.

Just as the initial call to Cornelius, "a devout man who feared God with all his household, gave alms liberally to the people, and prayed constantly to God" (Acts 10:2) was God's initiative, so also was the outpouring of the gift of the Holy Spirit. Cornelius had not seen such manifestations of the Holy Spirit and probably had not heard of them. Apparently, Peter had not even considered the possibility that these pagans might receive the Holy Spirit just as the Jewish Christians had. God amazed them all, gentile and Jew, by bestowing the Holy Spirit with the gift of tongues and praising God. The presence of the Holy Spirit convinced Peter to baptize these first gentile converts and bring them into full fellowship in the Church.

This event provoked a problem in the Church when the Jewish Christians in Jerusalem heard that Peter had eaten with uncircumcised men (Acts 11:1-3). The assumption of this group in the Church was that the new converts were not part of the covenant people, Israel, since they did not have circumcision, the sign of the covenant with Abraham. They also assumed that they worshiped pagan deities and ate unclean food — all of which were reasons for Jews to avoid any table fellowship with them.

 Stop here and read **Acts 11:12-17** in your own Bible.

Peter's first point is that the Spirit instructed him to go to Cornelius' house. His second point is that the Holy Spirit fell upon the gentiles just as it had on the Jewish Christians on Pentecost. Third, he mentions here that he remembered the words of the Lord Jesus promising that they would "be baptized with the Holy Spirit," a reference to Acts 1:5. This also brings out Jesus' teaching at the Last

Supper that the Holy Spirit would "bring to your remembrance all that I have said to you" (Jn 14:26). Finally, he recognized his own insignificance in regard to God's initiative, and therefore he could not "withstand God" by withholding baptism (Acts 11:17). The community in Jerusalem is silenced and then praises God for bringing the gentiles to repentance.

Mission to the World

Their amazement and discomfort with the conversion of the gentiles would continue for a number of years, and the Jewish Christians would come to accept the gentile Christians along difficult stages of development. The first of these was the evangelization of gentiles by Jewish Christians from the island of Cyprus and the city of Cyrene in Libya. These Jewish Christians who had grown up in the gentile world were at ease with the idea of preaching to non-Jews, with whom they were comfortable as neighbors. In the primarily gentile city of Antioch, Syria, many gentiles converted, causing enough discomfort among the Jerusalem Christians again that they sent Barnabas to check on it and take it to another level.

 Stop here and read **Acts 11:20-26** in your own Bible.

First, Barnabas was pleased by what he saw because he could recognize that the conversions were the action of the grace of God. Second, he sent for Saul, who had returned to his home city of Tarsus, which is not so far from Antioch. Saul came from a gentile environment and knew the Greek language and many of the gentile customs. Together they taught a large group of people. The important point behind all this is that Barnabas, the emissary from the nervous Jerusalem Jewish Christian church, was "a good man, full of the Holy Spirit and of faith" (Acts 11:24). His own goodness, plus the gifts of faith and the Holy Spirit, enabled him to discern the actions of God in Antioch and promote the good that God was doing. Because of this, the early mixed Christian community of gentiles and Jews in

Antioch were called "Christians," a title that has remained with the Church ever since (Acts 11:26).

CONSIDER

The Power of the Spirit

From Acts 2 through 11, Peter experienced the Holy Spirit guiding his words as he spoke. He was well aware of the difference between his fear at Gethsemane and Caiaphas' court, when he ran and denied even knowing Jesus, to Pentecost and beyond, when he boldly preached Jesus outside the upper room and stood up against the whole Sanhedrin twice. Therefore, we see the recognition of the role of the Holy Spirit in evangelizing: "It was revealed to them that they were serving not themselves but you, in the things which have now been announced to you by those who preached the good news to you through the Holy Spirit sent from heaven, things into which angels long to look" (1 Pet 1:12).

Not only does preaching come through the Holy Spirit who enables it, but also the Good News that is proclaimed presents mysteries of the faith that amaze even the angels. The empowerment to speak accompanies the depths of truth into which only the Holy Spirit of truth can direct people. By this, both the listeners and the Christian speakers are amazed.

The Holy Spirit not only continued to inspire the Church in Antioch to evangelize Jews and gentiles but also to take the Gospel beyond Antioch to the ends of the earth, as Jesus had commanded the apostles just before his ascension.

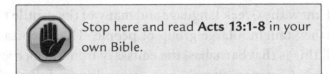 Stop here and read **Acts 13:1-8** in your own Bible.

The manner in which the Holy Spirit spoke to the worshiping community was through the prophets named in verse 1. The content of his words through those prophets was to set apart the two men who had already been taking leadership in the evangelization of the gentiles at Antioch — Barnabas and Saul — to take up the work to which the Holy Spirit has "called them" (Acts 13:2). This was not their own initiative but God's, just as was the case when the Holy Spirit guided Peter to evangelize and baptize the first gentile convert, Cornelius.

We also see that after fasting and prayer, "they laid their hands" on Barnabas and Saul to commission them for their apostolate (Acts 13:3). Just as the deacons were ordained after prayer and the laying on of hands, so were Barnabas and Saul ordained. Later, they would be able to ordain other men to become priests and bishops, key links in the 2,000-year-long chain of sacramental life, passing on Christ's spiritual authority through prayer and the laying on of hands.

They made the short journey from Antioch to Seleucia, which was the port city for Antioch, and sailed to the nearby large island of Cyprus. They preached throughout the island until they were confronted by a Jewish magician called Elymas bar-Jesus. He was a friend of the Roman proconsul, Sergius Paulus, and tried to prevent the governor from believing in Jesus Christ.

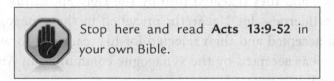

Stop here and read **Acts 13:9-52** in your own Bible.

At this point of direct opposition from a magician, the Holy Spirit fills Saul (who begins to use the Greek name "Paul") in order to confront the evil man directly. The Holy Spirit empowers him both to convict the man of his wickedness — being an enemy of righteousness, full of deceit and distortion of the Lord's ways — and to punish him temporarily by a blindness that makes him dependent on other people to lead him. Paul, who also experienced temporary blindness at the moment of his conversion, proclaims a punishment that will demonstrate the weakness of Elymas' so-called magical powers and perhaps motivate him, as well as the bystanders, to turn away from his false spirituality.

This can well be understood as a demonstration in power of Jesus' teaching that the Holy Spirit of truth would "convict" the world about sin, righteousness, and judgment. As a result, the proconsul Sergius Paulus becomes a Christian, and Paul and Barnabas sail from Cyprus to Perga, a river port in Asia Minor (modern Turkey) with access to the sea, and then they go farther inland and upland to Antioch of Pisidia, where Paul is invited to preach about Jesus in the local synagogue. The success of the sermon leads to a second invitation, which draws a huge crowd, inciting the leaders to jealousy and a persecution. At this point, Paul and Barnabas leave the city.

While seeming to have failed, the disciples experience a joy and the presence of the Holy Spirit, not a sense of failure or tragedy. In fact, they are experiencing the same pattern of ministry as Jesus himself experienced. Just as the Holy Spirit came upon Jesus at the Jordan, so Paul and Barnabas received the Holy Spirit in a new way by the prayer and imposition of hands that commissioned them at Antioch. Just as Jesus was confronted by Satan with temptations in the wilderness, so were the disciples by the magician Elymas in Cyprus, and they defeated him by the Holy Spirit. Just as Jesus left the wilderness for Nazareth, preached in the synagogue, and was first accepted and then rejected for his teaching, so were Paul and Barnabas accepted by the synagogue community in Antioch of Pisidia and then rejected.

The Holy Spirit is powerfully present throughout this pattern in both the mission of Jesus and his disciples. Yet, he also allows people their freedom to choose or reject Jesus and his Gospel, either for their rise or their fall. Similar patterns will apply to each of us, whether in relation to our own personal reaction to the Gospel or in the results of our mission to the world. With the latter situation, this parallel between Jesus and Paul applies to us. We can still experience the joy of the Holy Spirit even in times of seeming failure or rejection, because it is not about us; the issue is how people with free will respond to the promptings of the Holy Spirit in regard to Jesus Christ.

The Presence of the Holy Spirit

Paul traveled to the great city of Ephesus, the capital of the Roman province of Asia Minor, and began a long mission. Upon his arrival, he came upon twelve disciples, but he detected that the disciples there had never even heard there was a Holy Spirit, much less received the Spirit.

 Stop here and read **Acts 19:1-7** in your own Bible.

The text gives no explanation of why Paul asks if they have received the Holy Spirit, but he does ask. Through a series of questions, he discovers that they have received the baptism of repentance, from John, and this, as John and Jesus both said, is not able to communicate the Holy Spirit (see above). At this juncture, Paul explains that Jesus was the one whose coming John had predicted, which led them to let Paul baptize them in the name of Jesus, upon which they received the Holy Spirit. As with Cornelius, these Christians manifest the presence of the Holy Spirit within themselves by speaking in tongues and prophesying.

The Acts of the Apostles makes clear that the Gospel prospered in the early Church because of the power of the Holy Spirit being poured upon the Church and manifesting himself through the members in both preaching and miracles. Not only was Luke, the author of Acts, aware of this but so were the early Christians. Paul explicitly taught that he depended on the Holy Spirit in his ministry from the very beginning of his writings and emphasized the power of the Holy Spirit and his effects on spiritual Christian believers.

 Stop here and read **1 Corinthians 2:10-15** in your own Bible.

Paul begins his argument by stating that God revealed the truth to him through the Holy Spirit: Paul is not the great one who invented the teaching of Christ but someone who simply received it from the Holy Spirit. Then he establishes that the Holy Spirit searches even the "depths of God" (1 Cor 2:10) and his thoughts. Since Paul has received this Spirit rather than the world's spirit, the Spirit enables Paul to understand the gifts from God and to impart them in words taught by the Holy Spirit. If any of Paul's listeners are unspiritual, they will not be able to perceive these truths; the spiritual people in the crowds will perceive them. Paul is therefore forcing those who hear him to either accept all that the Holy Spirit teaches in power or to admit that they are unspiritual and ignorant of God. He explains that the gift of the Holy Spirit is not an external thing but rather a seal within the heart or soul of a person, working from the inside to shape the external words and actions.

Paul denies that his accomplishments are his own work, but the ministry is God's accomplishment. The ministry is for a "new covenant," as promised in Jeremiah 31:31 — "I will make a new covenant with the house of Israel and the house of Judah" — which Jesus fulfilled in his own blood. This new covenant in the Spirit will give life and will be filled with a righteousness of greater splendor than the old covenant at Sinai.

Paul also indicates that the Holy Spirit is the source of his virtues. Therefore, rather than hide his weaknesses as some type of failure, he boasts that the Holy Spirit works through it all.

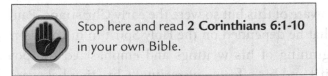

Stop here and read **2 Corinthians 6:1-10** in your own Bible.

When Paul's three-year ministry in Ephesus came to an end, he began a fateful journey to celebrate the feast of Pentecost in Jerusalem in the spring of A.D. 58. He wrote his Epistle to the Romans at this time to introduce himself to that community, in anticipation of a visit to that church, so that he might lay out the key points of his teaching. Toward the end of the letter, he reflects on his ministry up to that point, as is described in Acts. Of course, he writes of the power of the Holy Spirit when describing his ministry.

 Stop here and read **Romans 15:14-20** in your own Bible.

First, Paul clearly understands that he is able to be "a minister of Christ Jesus" only because of the grace he has received from God, and not because of his abilities. He understands this as a "priestly service" (Rom 15:16) — literally meaning, from the Greek, "doing what a priest does," even when he calls himself a "minister of Christ." In addition, Paul sees this priestly service as making "acceptable" the "offering of the Gentiles" (Rom 15:16). Paul's choice of terms here is amazing, since he was born of the tribe of Benjamin and was ineligible to be a Jewish priest, who could only be chosen from the family of Aaron of the tribe of Levi. Yet he explicitly recognizes the apostolic ministry as priestly. This can have two senses: first, he is offering up the gentiles to God as a pleasing sacrifice by their conversion to Christ; two, since all Christians are to "present your bodies as a living sacrifice, holy and acceptable to God, which is your spiritual worship" (Rom 12:1), his ministry serves to make them more acceptable people by helping them grow in holiness, virtue, and loving relationship with God.

Second, the gentiles are acceptable to God as an offering because the Holy Spirit has sanctified them. Though Paul's priestly ministry is by God's grace, the conversion, growth, and maturity in Christ is the work of the Holy Spirit within each Christian.

Third, even though Paul is proud of what he has done in his ministry to the gentiles, he explicitly recognizes that Christ has worked "through" him by word and deed and "by the power of the Holy Spirit" (Rom 15:19). Neither his priestly ministry, preaching and teaching in words, nor good deeds and miracles are based in his personal power but rather in God's action in Jesus Christ by the Holy

135

Spirit. Such an understanding is clearly demonstrated throughout Acts, and it is presented as a model for the understanding of every Christian ministry and service to preach the Gospel in the world.

STUDY

Power in the Spirit's Gifts

The power of the Holy Spirit is seen in bold preaching, healing, and some miracles. However, some episodes have mentioned two other gifts of the Holy Spirit — speaking in tongues and prophecy. Paul teaches about these gifts in three different passages.

The first teaching on the gifts of the Holy Spirit is in 1 Corinthians. There the problem is that some people had begun boasting about the superiority of their gifts, and they became yet another source division within that rather contentious community.

 Stop here and read **1 Corinthians 12:4-31** in your own Bible.

The first part of this teaching brings out a Trinitarian aspect, identifying the gifts as having their source in the three Persons of the one God — "the same Spirit" and "the same Lord," referring to Jesus Christ; and "the same God," referring to the Father (1 Cor 12:4-6). Paul's point is that the gifts are not given as a cause of division because they all derive from the same Lord God — Father, Son, and Spirit cooperating together, in the harmony the Christian community needs to manifest.

The second part brings out points about the purpose and the diversity of the gifts of the Holy Spirit. Paul lists eight different gifts, but emphasizes that each is given for the common good. The gifts are not given to augment the ego of any one member by claiming a superior ability. Rather, the gifts of the Holy Spirit are meant to strengthen the other members of the Church and to evangelize those who are outside the faith. To emphasize this, Paul will expound on the importance of love as the greatest of gifts, along with faith and hope, in 1 Corinthians 13.

The third section develops Paul's doctrine of the Church as the Mystical Body of Christ, emphasizing that each part of the body needs the other parts, even the humble parts, without which the whole body cannot function.

The fourth section lists the gifts again, but identifies them as being appointed by God, by whom Paul means the Father. Note that this list contains some gifts not mentioned in the first list (apostles, teachers, helpers, administrators) and omits others (word of knowledge, word of wisdom). The importance of this is to show that no list of the gifts of the Holy Spirit is exhaustive. Each omits some gifts and contains others. The Church is, therefore, open to a wide variety of gifts, some of which are manifested in the distinctive charisms of the hundreds of religious orders throughout the Church.

The Holy Spirit and Spiritual Warfare

The Holy Spirit had led Jesus to be tempted by the devil and defeat him, and Jesus cast out demons by the Holy Spirit. When Paul arrived in Cyprus, he engaged in a type of spiritual combat with the magician Elymas and defeated him by the Holy Spirit. These and other examples show that spiritual warfare against Satan and his demons requires the power of the Holy Spirit, as Paul teaches in Ephesians.

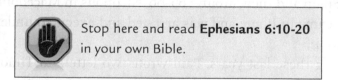

Stop here and read **Ephesians 6:10-20** in your own Bible.

In the first part, Paul wants Christians to understand that the need for spiritual strength derives from the fact that our battle is ultimately against the devil and his various levels of evil spirits — the principalities, powers, and world rulers "of this present darkness" (Eph 6:12). Though Christians might see human beings as their enemies in the flesh, behind them are the "spiritual hosts of wickedness" (Eph 6:12), who use people they have tempted into sin, and through sin to their subjugation.

The second part describes the armor and weaponry of this spiritual battle. The armor is for defensive purposes, and in spiritual battle it is the various gifts of God: the truth; righteousness to protect the heart like a breastplate; the Gospel of peace that keeps one marching to battle-like conflicts; faith, which protects one like a shield from arrows; and salvation, which protects the mind. The only offensive weapons are gifts of the Spirit — the word of God, which acts like a sword. The other is prayer and supplication "in the Spirit" (Eph 6:18). The Holy Spirit teaches us to pray as we ought, and Paul calls all Christians to pray much for one another and for help in this great spiritual combat.

 Stop here and read **Acts 28** in your own Bible.

The Acts of the Apostles ends rather inconclusively in the year A.D. 62, with Paul finally in Rome awaiting trial before the emperor, who at that time was Nero. The most logical reason for Luke not relating the outcome of the trial is that at the time of his writing he did not yet know. Apparently, Paul was set free, since Nero had not yet begun his persecution of the Church. He apparently did a mission in Spain and then, around 65-66, Nicopolis in Macedonia. After that, he came to Rome and was arrested and executed under Nero's persecution.

During these last years, Paul wrote two letters to Timothy and one to Titus, with Luke probably acting as his secretary (as evidenced by the vocabulary distinctive to these letters and to Luke-Acts). One final mention of the Holy Spirit's power in the ministry is appropriate for this lesson:

> Hence I remind you to rekindle the gift of God that is within you through the laying on of my hands; for God did not give us a spirit of timidity but a spirit of power and love and self-control. (2 Tim 1:6-7)

The gift of God possessed by Timothy, who was the bishop of Ephesus, was his ordination through the laying on of Paul's hands. This gift was capable of being "rekindled," the Greek word meaning to stir a fire back into flame after it had become a hot ember. Even when the gift seems to be low-key and just a burning ember, that does not mean it is doomed to be extinguished, because the Holy Spirit can always stir the gift back into the hot flame of "power and love and self-control." This applies to all clergy throughout the ages, who have received their ordination as a gift of the Holy Spirit — and it applies to all the lay faithful, who received their Sacrament of Confirmation by the laying on of hands.

No one has received a "spirit of timidity"; all have received the Holy Spirit and "fire" from God the Father through Jesus Christ our Lord. Yet we, too, cooperate with this gift, stir it up, and allow the Holy Spirit to blow it into a hot flame. The world needs this fire of the Holy Spirit today as much as the Palestine of Jesus and the Mediterranean world of Paul did in their day.

DISCUSS

1. List at least three gifts of the Spirit that are mentioned in the New Testament. Which of these do you consider the most important? Why?
2. How does the Spirit work in the New Testament? Does he work the same way today? Why or why not?
3. Talk about some of the ways Paul talks about the Spirit. How do those ways compare to the ways Old Testament figures understood the Lord's Spirit in their lives?

PRACTICE

Choose one verse from St. Paul's writing about the Holy Spirit and memorize it. Ask the Spirit to reveal himself to you in a special way this week. Make notes of any "coincidences" or "occurrences" which would show his presence in your life.

Session 7

THE SPIRIT AND THE SPIRITUAL LIFE

 "We can study the whole history of salvation, we can study the whole of Theology, but without the Spirit we cannot understand. It is the Spirit that makes us realize the truth or — in the words of Our Lord — it is the Spirit that makes us know the voice of Jesus."

— POPE FRANCIS, Homily (April 28, 2015)

The heavenly Father pours out the Holy Spirit through Jesus, his Son, and he affects the Christian life in many ways. This lesson will examine Scripture passages that describe his effects on the sacramental life, the virtues, prayer, and other aspects of Christian existence.

STUDY

The Holy Spirit and Baptism

During a nighttime visit to Jesus, the Pharisee Nicodemus opened the discussion with a recognition that Jesus is a "teacher come from God" (Jn 3:2). As in all of his discourses in John's Gospel, Jesus took him deeper, to the key question of being able to see the kingdom of God through a new birth.

 Stop here and read **John 3:3-8** in your own Bible.

Jesus introduces Nicodemus to a teaching that every human being must understand: the present level of existence in the world is a lower, "fleshly" existence, but the kingdom of God is the goal of life. The "flesh" refers to that aspect of human existence from which comes those lower desires and feelings that drag a person toward immorality and eventual spiritual and physical decay. In later centuries, Augustine and other theologians refer to it as our fallen human nature that experiences concupiscence — that is, the disordered desires for too much of some good things or too little of others. All of creation remains good as God has created it, but humans misuse the goodness for self-centered purposes and commit sin. Like other people of his time, Jesus calls this the "flesh," a reference to the easy corruption of physical meat, especially in hot climates. Jesus' antidote is being "born anew" (Jn 3:3), which can also be quite correctly translated as "born from above" (the Greek prefix *ana* can be either translated by "above" or by "again"), by water and the Spirit. Jesus then states that this rebirth takes place by being "born of water and the Spirit" (Jn 3:5), his first teaching on the meaning of Baptism.

John's baptism was primarily an expression of the candidate's repentance of former sin and was a turning away from a sinful past. However, John knew that he baptized merely with water and not with the Holy Spirit. He promised that Jesus would baptize with the Spirit and with fire. Here in John 3:5, Jesus states the same principle: the Holy Spirit is the power underlying his baptism, and not primarily the human being's act of repentance. In addition, while John's baptism by water alone was simply a turning away from sin, Jesus' baptism in water and the Holy Spirit is a turn toward eternal life and entrance into the "kingdom of God."

Baptize All Nations

 Stop here and read **Matthew 28:18-20** in your own Bible.

Though this passage does not make any point about the specific role of the Holy Spirit in Baptism, it is important to see that the baptismal formula Jesus gave his disciples was "in the name of the Father and of the Son and of the Holy Spirit" (Mt 28:19), a formula which has been standard among most Christians. The point relevant to our study is to see that inclusion of the Holy Spirit. Paul will teach that all three Persons cooperate in bestowing the power of Baptism, a truth that follows logically from Jesus' baptismal formula, "in the name," which is a singular noun that teaches the oneness of God, "of the Father and of the Son and of the Holy Spirit," three co-equal Persons in the one God.

Paul on the Holy Spirit in Baptism

Paul offers rich teachings on Baptism in a number of places, but three of them mention the role of the Holy Spirit's power to transform Christians from scattered sinners into the redeemed members united in the Church.

The first passage begins with a statement about the contrast of a sinful life with the life of baptized Christians.

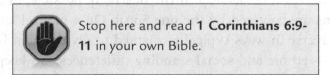

Stop here and read **1 Corinthians 6:9-11** in your own Bible.

The opening line here states one of the most basic principles of the spiritual life: the unrighteous will not inherit the kingdom of God. Paul never explicitly threatens anyone with hell, but he does state that the sinners will not go to heaven, so draw your own conclusions. To make the point clear, he lists a number of sins, concluding that the people who commit these sins will not inherit the kingdom of God, just in case anyone was unclear about this. An important point is that he is writing this to Christians who have already accepted Jesus and have been baptized. If he needs to warn them about this, then it must be possible for them to fall back into sin and lose the redemption Christ has given them.

He then teaches about baptism, which he describes as being "washed" (1 Cor 6:11). Baptism has the power to sanctify and justify those who accept it. Again, this is not a power that derives from their doing but from "the name of the Lord Jesus Christ" and the "Spirit of our God" (1 Cor 6:11). God the Father, Jesus, and the Holy Spirit fully cooperate in empowering Christian Baptism to make a person holy and justified. In so doing, a Christian can "inherit the kingdom of God," just as Jesus had taught.

The second passage on the Holy Spirit and the power of Baptism is also in 1 Corinthians:

> For just as the body is one and has many members, and all the members of the body, though many, are one body, so it is with Christ. For by one Spirit we were all baptized into one body — Jews or Greeks, slaves or free — and all were made to drink of one Spirit. (1 Cor 12:12-13)

In the context of teaching about the gifts of the Holy Spirit, Paul emphasizes that the diversity of spiritual gifts occurs within the one body of the Church that has Jesus Christ as its head. He teaches that Baptism makes membership in the one body possible, because all Christians are baptized by the one Spirit. On a natural level, people are diverse in ways typically oriented to divide them from one another — ethnic and social-standing differences can keep people isolated from one another. Paul makes the same point in his teaching on Baptism in Galatians: "For as many of you as were baptized into Christ have put on Christ. There is neither Jew nor Greek, there is neither slave nor free, there is neither male nor female; for you are all one in Christ Jesus" (Gal 3:27-28).

Natural differences that divide are irrelevant by our union in Christ, but not by mere human wishing them away. Rather, the Holy Spirit unites each Christian to Jesus Christ and through him to everyone else in his body, the Church.

The third of Paul's passages on Baptism and the Holy Spirit occurs in Titus, where he begins with the contrast between everyone's sinful past and the goodness of God that saved sinners by his mercy, not by their deeds.

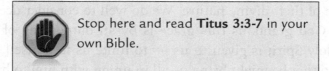

Stop here and read **Titus 3:3-7** in your own Bible.

Note that God's mercy enters sinners "by the washing of regeneration and renewal in the Holy Spirit" (Ti 3:5). Baptism, again, is this washing, and it is effective because of the power of the Holy Spirit, who gives "regeneration" (Ti 3:5) — that is, makes us "born again." This noun has the same root as the word Jesus gives for being born again in John 3:3. Regeneration (or rebirth) and renewal come in the Holy Spirit, just as Jesus taught. The Father pours out the Holy Spirit upon us "through Jesus Christ our Savior" (Ti 3:6), again showing that Baptism is an action of all three Persons of the Holy Trinity acting together.

CONSIDER

Access to the Father

Jesus revealed an important point about the inner life of the Blessed Trinity: Everything that the Holy Spirit has comes from Jesus, and Jesus receives it all from the Father. Now we can examine the other side of this truth as it affects our salvation and spiritual lives: "And he came and preached peace to you who were far off and peace to those who were near; for through him we both have access in one Spirit to the Father" (Eph 2:17-18).

Jesus is the one who "preached peace" to the "far off" gentiles and the nearby Jews, so as to grant peace and mercy to all people. Then Paul adds that through Jesus we have access to the Father "in one Spirit." This means that the Holy Spirit draws us to Jesus and unites us to him. Humans cannot make this happen on their own power, but the Holy Spirit works within the souls to effect this union. The purpose of union with Christ is that through and in Christ Jesus he unites us to the Father, since, as Jesus said, he and the Father "are one" (Jn 10:30), a reference to the one divine nature they share. We receive this union by grace; the Father, Son, and Holy Spirit have it by virtue of their divine nature. We do well to consider deeply that the way God grants us this grace is by an outpouring of himself — the Holy Spirit is given to us — to unite us to himself in Jesus Christ, so that he might bring us all in union with him to his union with the Father. Such is the goal of the holiness and righteousness that the Holy Spirit effects in our baptism.

The Spirit Reveals God's Truths

Jesus clearly taught that the Holy Spirit is the Paraclete, counseling us disciples and leading us to the truth, if we love Jesus and obey his commandments. This teaching remained very important not only for the eleven disciples who had heard Jesus teach at the Last Supper but also for Paul, his disciples (such as Timothy), and for the entire Church, on through the ages to the present. Our salvation is possible because the Holy Spirit "sanctifies" us — that is, he makes us holy. In that way, he affects the moral life. He also saves us by giving us faith in the truth, and not through any myths.

In his letter to the Ephesians, Paul wants the Ephesians to enter more deeply into the mystery of Christ by understanding his insights into it. He had written of "the revelation of the mystery" (Rom 16:25) and the way God "has made known to us in all wisdom and insight the mystery of his will" (Eph 1:9). He then states that this mystery

MYSTERY

Mystery, whether singular or plural, occurs twenty-three times in the New Testament. Four of them are in Revelation (1:20; 10:7; 17:5, 7), where the mystery comes from God (1:20; 10:7) or is a mystery of evil from the wicked Babylon (17:5, 7). All other occurrences are in Paul, mostly speaking about the mystery of God. The Aramaic word *razah* is used in the Aramaic sections of Daniel (2:19, 27, 30, 47; 4:9), referring to the king's dreams in both chapters. Daniel made it clear that only God could make the mystery known in Daniel 2, and King Nebuchadnezzar recognized in Daniel 4:9 that "the spirit of the holy gods" could make known all mysteries.

of Christ has been revealed "by the Spirit" (Eph 3:5), again following the promise of Christ that the Spirit of truth would lead the Church "into all the truth" (Jn 16:13). The import of this is that the gentiles and the Jews would become fellow heirs and partakers of the promise of the Gospel through receiving insight into the mystery of Jesus Christ. Clearly, the Holy Spirit is more than informative, drawing people to salvation through the knowledge he reveals.

In his Second Letter to Timothy, the bishop he left to care for the church in Ephesus, Paul understands that the Holy Spirit entrusts the truth to Timothy and Paul. This same Holy Spirit dwells within us and gives those truths that are necessary for the faith. Therefore, Paul charges Timothy to "guard" these truths (2 Tim 1:14). They cannot change because they are true. The truth that Timothy receives will be consistent with the "sound words" he had heard from Paul (2 Tim 1:13). Therefore, protect the truth.

 Stop here and read **2 Timothy 1:13-14** in your own Bible.

Paul's warning to protect the truth is necessary because some people will want to diverge from the truth. This also is a truth that the Holy Spirit made known, so Timothy, like Paul and the other apostles, must be ready for those who would change and pervert the truth of the faith. The falsehoods will at times come from "deceitful spirits" and "demons," while at other times people's consciences will be seared due to the evil of their behavior. They will try to deal with their own bad consciences by overreaction, prohibiting things that are good in themselves, like marriage and various foods. Though the Church has room for celibates like Paul and those who imitate Jesus' celibacy in religious life, marriage is always professed as a great good. Therefore, Timothy must be alert to the possibility of falsehoods and always remain faithful to the truth that was given by the Holy Spirit.

The ability to discern the true from the false is one of the gifts of the Holy Spirit mentioned in the list in 1 Corinthians 12:10: "the ability to distinguish between spirits." Knowledge of the Spirit of truth makes it possible to discern the false spirits that pose as Christian when in fact they, and the various false ideas about Jesus and the Gospel, are false.

At other points, Paul is convinced that he speaks the truth about various issues because the Holy Spirit has given it to him: for example, when he advises a widow to remain single after the death of her husband in 1 Corinthians 7:40. Yet, he also admits that she is free to remarry, so it is his personal judgment guided by the Holy Spirit.

STUDY

Knowledge and Gifts of the Spirit

While it is good to seek the gifts of the Holy Spirit, especially love, it remains good to use the other gifts, including that of speaking in tongues. However, this gift has a specific limitation: other people cannot understand the speaker, so it does them no particular good. One can only take the stance that one is speaking "mysteries in the Spirit" that only God can understand: "Make love your aim, and earnestly desire the spiritual gifts, especially that you may prophesy. For one who speaks in a tongue speaks not to men but to God; for no one understands him, but he utters mysteries in the Spirit" (1 Cor 14:1-2).

The better way of keeping love as one's aim or purpose is to be eager for those "manifestations of the Spirit" (1 Cor 14:12) that build up the whole Church. Speaking in tongues is good, but it has limited ability for building up the Christian life of other people. Therefore, it is good to use the mind and help other people spiritually.

Faith, Hope, and Love Come from the Holy Spirit

The Church identifies three virtues as theological: faith, hope, and love. These are necessary for humans to attain eternal salvation, but all three are free gifts given by God without humans ever being capable of earning the graces of these virtues. God bestows each of these virtues as his free gift, but humans can and must cooperate in accepting these graces as freely accepted by them. God establishes a relationship with each person who is willing to accept these virtues; their nature is to form an interpersonal relationship. The human partner in the loving faith relationship can perceive the benefit of these virtues in other people. As grace moves their will, they begin to ask for these graces and take steps to remove that which blocks them — which is usually the sins committed by the person. Still, ultimately, these are the action of God within the soul, and for that reason it is necessary to understand what the Scripture teaches on the role of the Holy Spirit in enabling humans to receive faith, hope, and charity.

Calling God "Father" and Jesus "Lord"

The Holy Spirit makes it possible for a person to make an act of faith by working within the heart and soul to accept the faithful, trusting relationship with God. The first step is a recognition that Jesus of Nazareth is Lord: "Therefore I want you to understand that no one speaking by the Spirit of God ever says 'Jesus be cursed!' and no one can say 'Jesus is Lord' except by the Holy Spirit" (1 Cor 12:3).

This act of faith is possible only with the help of the Holy Spirit. It marks a transition from seeing Jesus of Nazareth as a carpenter from a small village who was crucified as a criminal to accepting his glorious resurrection, his lordship over life, his conquest of sin and death, and his divinity — "My Lord and my God" (Jn 20:28), as Thomas professed. A human mind can evaluate the evidence about Jesus' life, death, and resurrection, but only the Holy Spirit can move the soul to accepting his Jesus' lordship over one's life.

A second step moves from accepting Jesus' lordship and an abstract notion of God the creator and sustainer of the universe to the kind of personal relationship that Jesus has, by which one relates to God as "Father." A few Old Testament texts consider God as a Father, but few individuals saw God as their own father. Jesus claimed a unique relationship with God as his Father, which caused him trouble, as when the people wanted to kill him because he "called God his Father, making himself equal with God" (Jn 5:18). In addition, Jesus taught his disciples to call God "Father" when they prayed (Mt 6:9; Lk 11:2), and he prayed that the name "Father" would keep them one: "Holy Father, keep them in your name, which you have given me, that they may be one, even as we are one" (Jn 17:11, RSV-SCE).

Paul reminds Christians that because they have accepted the lordship of Jesus, they have been redeemed from sin and have received adoption as God's children. Just as no one can call Jesus "Lord" without the Holy Spirit, neither can anyone accept the adoption and cry from his or her heart, "Abba, Father" (Rom 8:15; Gal 4:6). *Abba* is the Aramaic word for father, a familiar term still used in modern Hebrew by children addressing their fathers. The Holy Spirit enables a person to cry out this name to God and in so doing transforms people from slaves to sin into children and heirs of eternal life.

INVESTIGATE

GOD AS FATHER

 Look up the following passages and notice what the Scriptures say about the Spirit and the Father.

PASSAGE	NOTES
Romans 8:14-17	
Galatians 4:4-7	

STUDY

Faith and Hope

Faith is only the first of the theological virtues, and it is the basis for the others. Paul also connects the acts of faith that the Holy Spirit makes possible with acts of hope. Again, we need to pay attention to the fact that hope is a grace that the Holy Spirit makes possible, but he gives that grace in a relationship with people by which each person must respond with an act of acceptance of the grace. We see this in Paul's prayer for the Roman community toward the end of his epistle: "May the God of hope fill you with all joy and peace in believing, so that by the power of the Holy Spirit you may abound in hope" (Rom 15:13).

Paul offers a prayer that "the God of hope" may fill them with joy and peace in believing. Accepting faith in Jesus Christ and drawing close to him in a commitment of faith brings joy and peace as a result of faith. People who seek joy and peace usually miss it; joy and peace are effects from faith, not the cause of faith. He offers this prayer because he recognizes that faith and hope come from the Holy Spirit's power.

Modern people often need to distinguish hope from optimism. Optimism is based on human ideas, philosophies, and plans, and has frequently instigated some of the worst catastrophes in human history — the liberalism of the French Revolution and Napoleonic Wars; nationalism by Bismarck, leading to the Franco-Prussian War and World War I; racist nationalism linked to National Socialism (Nazism) and fascism in World War II; and Marxist atheism. All of these ideas appealed to people because they promised an ideal society. Inevitably, these ideologies collapsed in violence and destruction, giving rise to pessimism among the people, who were forced to survive in the wreckage of personal lives, entire countries, and cultures.

Christian hope has eternal life with God in heaven as its ultimate goal. Such hope has enabled millions of Christians to endure persecution and horrible suffering, often at the hands of the very optimists who killed off people of faith. Though Christian hope is centered on the future life in heaven and, at the end of the world, the resurrection of the dead, such hope has also inspired Christians to make astounding contributions to life in this world: from the founding of monastery schools in the so-called Dark Ages and the establishment of universities in the Medieval Renaissance to the creation of the first hospitals, mental institutions, and orphanages. Christianity has inspired the development of science, the exploration of the world, and advances in philosophy and the foundations of capitalistic economic theories. The spread of beautiful art (for example, the Sistine Chapel), music, architecture, and literature is strongly influenced by Christian faith and its recognition of the dignity of human beings.

Paul also linked faith and hope with the Holy Spirit's outpouring of love into Christian hearts.

 Stop here and read **Romans 5:1-5** in your own Bible.

The first step in this passage is that faith in Jesus Christ justifies sinners, making them right before God by Jesus' self-offering on the cross and bestowing inner peace. This comes by grace, and we are able to "rejoice in our hope of sharing the glory of God" (Rom 5:2) — the grace of faith is the source of hope for glory. This hope that looks forward to the glory of heaven makes it possible to "rejoice in our sufferings" in this life (Rom 5:3). The reason is that hope looks forward to a process by which suffering leads to endurance, character, and even more hope. This increase of hope that comes through the struggles and difficulties of life is able to provide a satisfaction because through it all the same Holy Spirit, whose power makes hope possible, also fills human hearts with God's love. This love is not mere human affection but rather the same quality of self-giving that characterizes God's love.

Again we see that through the Holy Spirit, all three theological virtues are effective in human life: "For through the Spirit, by faith, we wait for the hope of righteousness. For in Christ Jesus neither circumcision nor uncircumcision is of any avail, but faith working through love" (Gal 5:5-6).

The starting principle in this verse is that the virtues come through the Holy Spirit. Again, the first step is faith in Jesus Christ's redemption. That faith is the basis upon which we can "wait for the hope of righteousness." Interestingly, righteousness, also translated with the Latin root "justification," is an object of hope. That means we may not have gotten it yet, but faith gives us hope for a fullness of righteousness. Finally, it is the faith given by the Holy Spirit, a faith that works itself out in love, that matters. The works of the Law — that is, the Old Testament Torah — do not save a person. However, Paul does not reject all "works"; faith works itself out in love, and that is also the gift of the same Holy Spirit.

Paul adds another element to the Holy Spirit's role in giving us the theological virtues of faith and love when he teaches the Ephesians that the Holy Spirit strengthens the "inner man" so that Christ can dwell within us by faith and that we might be "rooted and grounded in love" (Eph 3:16, 17).

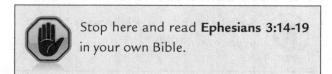

Stop here and read **Ephesians 3:14-19** in your own Bible.

This passage assumes that the inner man is not strong enough for Christ to dwell within us through faith or for us to be grounded in love. Nor can humans strengthen themselves to receive Christ's presence. This is a strengthening accomplished within us by the Holy Spirit by his "might," not by human might (Eph 3:16). Only by the power of the Holy Spirit will Christians be able to comprehend "the breadth and length and height and depth" of God's mysteries, or "know the love of Christ which surpasses knowledge," or "be filled with all the fullness of God" (Eph 3:18, 19). The Christian life is an invitation in faith, hope, and love to be engaged by the infinite mystery of God, and only the Holy Spirit, who searches the "depths of God," enables mere humans to do that.

Source of Love

The Holy Spirit is also the source of love.

 Stop here and read **Colossians 1:3-8** in your own Bible.

Here Paul recognizes that the Colossians' faith in Christ Jesus and love for all the other members of the Church ("the saints") are the result of their hope in heaven (Col 1:4). They can see that beyond this life is a heaven with God, so they believe in him now, and they love now, since love will characterize the life of heaven. He is explicit in recognizing that this love is "in the Spirit" (Col 1:8), possessing a power to love others that is beyond any mere human capacity.

Paul also taught that hope gives courage in the face of difficult dangers by which he could trust that the Holy Spirit will be able to deliver him from imprisonment and execution.

 Stop here and read **Philippians 1:19-20** in your own Bible.

At this point of Paul's imprisonment, perhaps in Caesarea Maritima, from A.D. 58 to late 60, he believes himself to be in danger of being executed. While he trusts that the Holy Spirit can get him out of this difficulty, Paul is still able to trust that Jesus Christ will receive honor, whether he survives or dies.

CONSIDER

The Holy Spirit and Other Virtues

In some places, Paul writes about the need of the Holy Spirit as the source of power for various virtues. For instance, "zeal" in serving the Lord flows from the Holy Spirit in Romans 12:11: "Never flag in zeal, be aglow with the Spirit, serve the Lord."

He also identifies life in the "kingdom of God" as "righteousness and peace and joy in the Holy Spirit" that makes a Christian pleasing to God through this action of God's gracious gift within the soul in Romans 14:17-18.

Paul summons the Ephesians to "lead a life worthy" of their calling as Christians (Eph 4:1). By this, he means a life of virtue, beginning with humility — in lowliness and meekness. A humble person does not need to insist on his own privilege or rights and therefore can display "patience" and "forbearing ... in love" (Eph 4:2). This kind of patience is not that of weakness but of the strength that flows from loving another person in self-giving.

 Stop here and read **Ephesians 4:1-5** in your own Bible.

Within this "worthy" life of virtue lived out in love, it becomes clearer that Christians are to have the one and same hope and faith, since the Spirit, the Lord Jesus, and the Father — who bestow hope, faith and love — are one God. Furthermore, Baptism "in the name of the Father and of the Son and of the Holy Spirit" is one that makes people members of the one Body of Christ. Therefore, the unity for which Jesus prayed to the Father — "that they be one, even as we are one" (Jn 17:11) — is the model for life in the Church.

STUDY

Desires of the Flesh and Desires of the Spirit

Paul takes more time in Galatians to develop his idea of walking "by the Spirit" rather than gratifying "the desires of the flesh" (Gal 5:16). This is a classic example of the term "flesh" referring to that aspect of human life that causes decay — physical and moral. He lays out an opposition between the "desires of the flesh" and the "desires of the Spirit" (Gal 5:17). This text requires us to both pay close attention to these two antagonistic forces within us and to decide to choose the life-giving qualities of the Spirit over against the flesh.

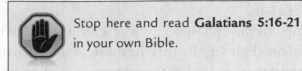

Stop here and read **Galatians 5:16-21** in your own Bible.

Paul lists the works of the flesh, and we need to pay close attention to their wide diversity. As expected of the desires of the flesh, various sexual sins make this list — fornication, impurity, licentiousness — along with drunkenness and carousing. However, the sins also include false religion — idolatry and sorcery — which include the various forms of occult and magical practices still popular today: astrology, séances, and spirit channeling — along with a pagan revival. The other sins of the flesh can be committed without any physical or bodily involvement, and instead by the mind and the will: enmity, strife, jealousy, anger, selfishness, dissension, factionalism, and envy. These sins are all so evil that they can exclude a person from inheriting the kingdom of God.

The other side of this spiritual and moral conflict is the "fruit of the Spirit" (Gal 5:22).

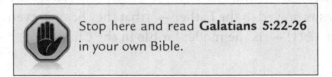

Stop here and read **Galatians 5:22-26** in your own Bible.

This list begins with the theological virtue of love but goes on to include a wide variety of virtues that flow from love. These virtues do not naturally grow from the flesh. In fact, Paul warns us that "those who belong to Christ Jesus" — that is, those who by the Holy Spirit recognize him as Lord, "crucify," or put to death, "the flesh with its passions and desires" (Eph 5:24). That is what he means by *living* and *walking* "by the Spirit" (Gal 5:25) — dying to oneself, dying to conceit and envy and to all the works of the flesh so that the fruit of the Spirit can grow within us.

Another interesting point on the term "fruit of the Spirit" vs. "gifts of the Spirit": The gifts can be handed to a person, and over time one learns how to use them. Fruit, on the other hand, grows slowly. It begins as a blossom that is immediately beautiful and smells sweet. Often, new converts find an immediate peace and joy as they make some initial changes in their moral and spiritual life. However, blossoms inevitably fall away, leaving a small, green, bitter nub. The next step of spiritual progress can seem like that nub and feel hard. Even as the fruit grows in size, it remains green and bitter, moving to a stage of being sour — then it acquires color, and only lastly does it become sweet. So also is the process of spiritual and moral growth in the fruit of the Spirit — hard and bitter for a while, but sweet and delightful by the end.

INVESTIGATE

OPPOSITION OF FLESH AND SPIRIT

Galatians 5 is not the only place where Paul describes the opposition of the flesh and the Spirit. Look up the following passages and make notes on the flesh vs. the Spirit.

PASSAGE	NOTES
Romans 7:14-25	
Romans 7:25	

Roman 8:1-8	
Galatians 6:8-9	

The "just requirement of the law" can be fulfilled as the law of God should be fulfilled only if we "walk" "according to the Spirit" and "not according to the flesh." The way of the flesh seeks only those things of the flesh that lead to its corruption and death, hostility to God, and a refusal to please God. The life "according to the Spirit" considers the "things of the Spirit" and leads one to "life and peace" (Rom 8:5-6).

Paul reminds Christians that if indeed the Spirit of God does dwell within them, they are no longer "in the flesh" (Rom 8:9). The same Holy Spirit of the Father who raised Jesus from the dead will give eternal life to their mortal bodies. And finally, they are no longer in debt to the flesh and need not fear death, because the Holy Spirit puts the flesh and its deeds to death and promises eternal life.

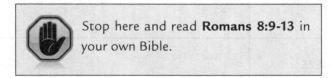 Stop here and read **Romans 8:9-13** in your own Bible.

Both Galatians 5 and Romans 8 offer tremendous hope for the Christian who turns away from the way of the flesh that leads to corruption and ultimate death and, instead, walks in the way of the

Spirit and has hope for eternal life, as well as love, peace, and all the virtues during this life on earth.

STUDY

The Holy Spirit and Prayer

Jesus taught his disciples how to pray. The Our Father was given in response to the apostles asking him to teach them how to pray. At that point, he continued the teaching with an instruction on asking, seeking, and knocking with persistence for the Father's good things.

 Stop here and read **Luke 11:9-13** in your own Bible.

After using the example of a human father giving the necessary goods to a child, Jesus explains that the heavenly Father will give the Holy Spirit to "those who ask him" (Lk 11:13). Though the disciples have not asked about the Holy Spirit, Jesus teaches that he is the gift they can be sure to receive. Without further explanation, we can see this as a desired result of prayer and a preparation for Jesus' instructions immediately before his ascension, when the disciples are told to return to Jerusalem to "wait for the promise of the Father, which, he said, 'you heard from me, for John baptized with water, but before many days you shall be baptized with the Holy Spirit'" (Acts 1:4-5).

Worship in Truth

While walking through Samaria on his return from Jerusalem to Galilee, Jesus rests at "Jacob's well" while his disciples go into the town to procure food. In their absence, a woman comes at noon to draw water, and he begins a dialogue by asking her for a drink of water.

 Stop here and read **John 4:1-24** in your own Bible.

As the dialogue progresses, he reveals that she has had five husbands and that the present man is not her husband. After hearing this, she accepts that Jesus is a prophet. She abruptly changes the subject from her sins to theology, questioning whether the Samaritans or the Jews have the correct temple. Although Jesus says that "salvation is from the Jews," he takes her to the next step that "true worshipers will worship the Father in Spirit and truth" because "God is Spirit" (Jn 4:22-24). The Holy Spirit is the one working within the human spirit to enable a person to adore God, just as he operates within a person to enable them to say, "Jesus is Lord" and "Abba, Father." Such is the worship that the Father "seeks," and he gives the gift of the Spirit to enable humans to do the spiritual worship he seeks.

In Our Weakness

Paul also teaches that the Holy Spirit enables people to pray because we do not know "how to pray as we ought":

> Likewise the Spirit helps us in our weakness; for we do not know how to pray as we ought, but the Spirit himself intercedes for us with sighs too deep for words. And he who searches the hearts of men knows what is the mind of the Spirit, because the Spirit intercedes for the saints according to the will of God. (Rom 8:26-27)

Most people pray in the sense of offering petitions to God, particularly in moments of desperation and danger, and sometimes at moments of desire for things we do not need ("Lord, I sure would like that Ford F-350 [or a diamond].") However, humans are created with a longing for the infinite, for God himself (a truck or a ring can't satisfy that longing), and the Holy Spirit intercedes for us to find those deepest longings — freedom from sin, personal integrity, the discovery of the ultimate joy in God, and the purpose and meaning of life in this world, as well as hope for life after death.

The Holy Spirit does not guess at the true needs of human hearts. He who is "the Spirit of truth" "searches the hearts" and knows people's deepest desires better than they. Therefore "the Spirit intercedes for the saints according to the will of God" and not according to the limitations of human will and knowledge, thereby demonstrating that he is truly the Paraclete that offers true counsel and advocacy as we pray.

True Joy

In Ephesians, Paul teaches that the power of the Holy Spirit can replace the human attempts to find joy through inebriation with a true and lasting joy that offers joyful thanks to God in the community.

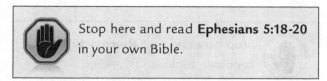

Stop here and read **Ephesians 5:18-20** in your own Bible.

Paul prohibits drunkenness as "debauchery" that brings down and destroys the soul, and he summons the Christian to be "filled with the Spirit" (Eph 5:18), so that the community might be able to pray in various ways, including singing praise and thanksgiving to the Lord with their whole hearts. The attempts to "get high" through alcohol, drugs, sex, or various other techniques are foolish, destructive, and even death-dealing imitations of the peace and joy that only God can grant. This is the reason that Paul commands all Christians to be filled with the Holy Spirit instead of the fake and destructive highs. The Holy Spirit evokes beauty from the human heart — poetic psalms, hymns, songs, and melodies. Without God, many people have a dark and hideous interior that they feel a need to express outwardly in order to be true to themselves. The Holy Spirit alters the dark with his light, the ugly with his beauty, and the hateful with love and truth. In this way, he leads people to the deepest longings that their own hearts are too polluted with sin, rejection, and loneliness to even recognize. He is the Paraclete that counsels their spiritual life to the truth, beauty, and goodness.

CONSIDER

Suffering by Believers

The fact that Christians may have the "first fruits of the Spirit" (Rom 8:23) does not exempt them from suffering in this world.

Christians have suffered loss and death for their faith in Jesus Christ from the first years of the Church, and the hatred has grown worse than ever in the twentieth and twenty-first centuries (40 million Christians have been martyred since 1915, out of the total 75 million martyrs in all of the Church's history). The reality of the world's ongoing rejection of Jesus Christ and Christianity reminds believers of the need for hope.

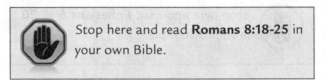

Stop here and read **Romans 8:18-25** in your own Bible.

Paul begins by evaluating the sufferings of this world: they are nothing compared to the glory of heaven, and the glory that each of the redeemed will become. Part of the virtue of hope is a contemplation of heaven as the truest goal of life. Christians also hope for the holiness and joy not yet seen in their lives — hope for an end of the vice and the injustice, as well as the suffering and the oppression, that plague their own souls and the world. Hope for eternity in heaven is not a desire to get the things and pleasures we missed while on earth but rather the direct vision of God: Father, Son, and Holy Spirit. The saints do not merely observe God but participate in the life of the Trinity. Like a baby who is fascinated with the loving look directly in the eyes by a mother or a father, so will we look into the infinite love that God has for us, a joyful love that transcends any earthly pleasure because it will not be interrupted by some other need or desire, by exhaustion or boredom. God's love will care for us beyond any care a parent, spouse, child, or friend could show. That is the hope that sustains Christians through any suffering or pang of loss or inadequacy we might feel.

Yet during this life, we experience an inward groaning, both because we become ever more aware of our need to grow in virtue and because we contrast the attitude of the world with the gifts and fruits of the Holy Spirit. We groan because of the world's rejection and persecution of believers precisely because they live in accord with the gifts and virtues poured out by the Holy Spirit. Still, in the midst of it all, we receive his grace to hope, and therefore "in this hope we were saved" (Rom 8:24), as the Holy Spirit sustains us until that point we receive that fullness of adoption as we inherit eternal life in heaven and, seeing God face-to-face, know the love that lasts forever.

Strength in Difficulties

Saul, the converted persecutor, fled a death threat in Damascus (Acts 9:23-25) and came to Jerusalem, where his preaching instigated another plot to kill him by the same Hellenist Jews who had killed Stephen. Therefore the Jerusalem community sent him to his hometown of Tarsus in Asia Minor, and the Church experienced a time of peace and growth.

 Stop here and read **Acts 9:26-31** in your own Bible.

The Church's peace and growth throughout Judea, Galilee, and Samaria was possible as the community walked "in the fear of the Lord," which is the beginning of wisdom and in the "comfort of the Holy Spirit" (Acts 9:31). Many people have difficulty understanding that fear of the Lord can bring peace, because they confuse or conflate this fear of the Lord with human anxiety. However, here the community begins with the wisdom that flows from fear of the Lord, and they easily find comfort in the Holy Spirit, even after having suffered their first persecution. Both fear of the Lord and the comfort of the Holy Spirit transcend mere human emotions, such as anxiety or satisfaction for accomplishments.

An example of that appears in 2 Corinthians 5, where Paul describes his anxiety while living in the present life. He is still living in Ephesus, where his enemies grow more bold and dangerous, but he can assure the Corinthians that the Holy Spirit was given to them as a guarantee of the hope and all other virtues that God will pour out upon them until the day they see God face-to-face.

Stop here and read **Acts 19:21-20:6** and **2 Corinthians 5:4-5** in your own Bible.

Transformed Life

The Holy Spirit transforms the entire religious life of the believing Christian. As Paul wrote about the Spirit's power to discharge us from the old law given by Moses to a new, interior code: "But now we are discharged from the law, dead to that which held us captive, so that we serve not under the old written code but in the new life of the Spirit" (Rom 7:6).

The Holy Spirit does not remove the moral law from Christians but lets morality deepen through an interior understanding and wisdom regarding the integration of truth, righteousness, and goodness into a profound understanding of human dignity. Already, Christians begin to live a "new life of the Spirit" because the moral law wells up from within them. Their faith, hope, and charity are not the struggles of intellectual grappling with the problems of human existence but flow from a deep relationship with the Person of the Holy Spirit. He draws out from the Christian a cry that "Jesus is Lord" and through Jesus we receive an adoption by which we can say to God, "Abba, Father," giving us an interpersonal relationship with the interpersonal God. Prayer is his gift, whether personal or communal. All of this and more is the "new life of the Spirit."

Finally, humans find authentic freedom — not from moral constraints as moderns would have it, but from sin and its destructive qualities and tendencies. This freedom from sin enables a Christian to behold the glory of the Lord, so that his glory can transform us sinners into glory.

Truly, all of this "comes from the Lord who is the Spirit" (2 Cor 3:18). Let us seek him as the primary gift of the Father and give him free rein to lead us into one glory after another in this life, and on into eternity.

DISCUSS

1. What are some specific ways the Holy Spirit empowers people to live a moral life?
2. Which gifts of the Spirit, as listed in 1 Corinthians 12, do you identify in your own life? What gift would you like to ask the Holy Spirit to give you?
3. What is the most significant new thought you've had about the Spirit in the course of this study?

PRACTICE

Take some time this week to examine your life for the gifts and fruits of the Spirit. Ask yourself how you can use these gifts and fruits to greater good in your family and the Church.

DISCUSS

1. What are some specific ways the Holy Spirit empowers people to live a moral life?
2. Which gifts of the Spirit, as listed in 1 Corinthians 12, do you identify in your own life? What gift would you like to ask the Holy Spirit to give you?
3. What is the most significant new thought you've had about the Spirit in the course of this study?

PRACTICE

Take some time this week to examine your life for the gifts and fruits of the Spirit. Ask yourself how you can use these gifts and fruits to greater good in your family and the Church.

VENI, CREATOR SPIRITUS

Come, Holy Spirit, Creator blest,
and in our souls take up Thy rest;
come with Thy grace and heavenly aid
to fill the hearts which Thou hast made.

O comforter, to Thee we cry,
O heavenly gift of God Most High,
O fount of life and fire of love,
and sweet anointing from above.

Thou in Thy sevenfold gifts are known;
Thou, finger of God's hand we own;
Thou, promise of the Father, Thou
Who dost the tongue with power imbue.

Kindle our sense from above,
and make our hearts o'erflow with love;
with patience firm and virtue high
the weakness of our flesh supply.

Far from us drive the foe we dread,
and grant us Thy peace instead;
so shall we not, with Thee for guide,
turn from the path of life aside.

Oh, may Thy grace on us bestow
the Father and the Son to know;
and Thee, through endless times confessed,
of both the eternal Spirit blest.

Now to the Father and the Son,
Who rose from death, be glory given,
with Thou, O Holy Comforter,
henceforth by all in earth and heaven. Amen.